BLESSED ARE YOU...
BECAUSE YOU HAVE BELIEVED

Robert S. Maloney, s.x.

Blessed are you...
because you have believed

Life of
Mother Celestine Healy-Bottego
Foundress of the Xaverian
Missionaries of Mary

EDITRICE MISSIONARIA ITALIANA

On the cover: reproduction of an original ceramic commissioned by Mother Bottego and produced by Scuola Beato Angelico, Milano, Italy, to adorn the tabernacle, Motherhouse Chapel, San Lazzaro, Parma, Italy.

© 2002 by Editrice Missionaria Italiana
All rights reserved
Published by EMI
via di Corticella, 181 - 40128 Bologna - Italy
Tel. 051/32.60.27 - Fax 051/32.75.52
web: http://www.emi.it
e-mail: sermis@emi.it

Printed in July 2002 by Grafica Universal
on behalf of GESP - Città di Castello (PG) - Italy

© 2002 EMI of Coop. SERMIS

N.A. 1807
ISBN 88-307-1169-1

PRESENTATION

IN KINDNESS AND IN TRUTH

My dear friends,

*With gratitude and joy, I present to you Fr. Robert S. Maloney's biography of **Madre Celestine Bottego**, beloved foundress of the Xaverian Missionaries of Mary. This fine book also chronicles the life of the **Saveriane** who have worked devotedly for over fifty years in their missions all over the world and for nearly fifty years in the Diocese of Worcester.*

Celestine, daughter of John and Mary (Healy) Bottego, born in Glendale, Ohio, raised in Butte, Montana, grew into a woman who opened her heart to the fire of the Holy Spirit. Her intense love for Christ was manifested in her love for His poor, His least ones - first in America and then in San Lazzaro, Parma - Italy, and ultimately, in many countries on several continents! Celestine's "fiat" to the call of Christ on May 24, 1944, led to the formal establishment of the Xaverian Missionaries of Mary some six years later. On July 2, 1950, on the "old" feast of the Visitation, Madre and the first three missionaries made their religious profession in the Chapel of Villa Bottego in Parma. Thus began a spiritual venture in bringing hope and healing and education in Christ's name to people in America, Brazil, Japan, Congo, Sierra Leone, Cameroun, Chad, Burundi, Thailand, and Mexico.

Madre Celestine was "born teacher," gifted with a loving heart, a profound faith, and remarkable courage, all the marks of a true missionary! She and her sisters have embraced the whole world in the name of Christ with the

Blessed Mother as their model of life and missionary spirit. Madre realized her spiritual dream - to be Christ for the lowly of the world, to uphold their dignity and honor their cultures, and to teach them the ways of the Lord while helping to make their lives better. Indeed, there is truth in what was written Madre when she came to visit a family in Parma. On her arrival, one of the family exclaimed: "Open the door! Here comes Celestine, the angel with big wings!"

We give thanks to God for Madre Celestine's splendid life in faith! We give thanks to God for all the Saveriane who continue Madre's mission in the grace of Christ the Lord who has called them always to be angels with big wings!

Finally, a special word of thanks to Fr. Robert S. Maloney for his loving tribute to this great woman of the Church.

Lord's blessings to all the Xaverian Missionaries of Mary!

Worcester, June 12, 2002

Sincerely yours in Christ,

+ Daniel P. Reilly

Most Reverend Daniel P. Reilly
Bishop of Worcester

PRESENTATION

I am very pleased to present this life of Mother Bottego, the foundress of the Missionaries of Mary, the feminine branch of the Xaverian Missionaries. With patient persistence the author, Fr. Robert S. Maloney, researched Mother's childhood years in America, and here presents previously unknown information and reflections regarding the first fifteen years of her life.

Mother Celestine Bottego was born in 1895 in the United States. Her father, John Bottego, had emigrated to America from his native Parma, Italy. He met and later married Mary Healy, the daughter of Irish parents who had come to America during the potato famine in their homeland.

Celestine lived and completed her grammar school studies in Butte, Montana. In 1910 she accompanied her mother to Italy, where her father and siblings had settled a few years earlier.

Father Maloney met mother in 1954 when he was still a seminarian. At that time Mother Bottego, "the foundress," had returned to the land of her birth, to established a community of the Missionaries of Mary, in the diocese of Worcester, Massachusetts. Father Maloney was deeply impressed by Mother. In later years and during his years as Vicar General of the Xaverian Missionaries, his admiration for this exceptional woman grew, and his interest in her life made this biography possible. We are pleased to make this life story available to people in America and elsewhere with whom Mother reserved profound family, cultural and spiritual ties.

From her mother Mother Celestine inherited her quick Irish humor, and her ability to serenely smile in the face of all of the difficulties or contrarieties of life. Her years in the western United States taught her to welcome people of various cultures and religions. She learned early how to dialog, establish lasting relationships with peoples of different social status. Her family status never impeded her from reaching out to the poor and sharing whatever she had with the needy.

Her constant union with the Lord enabled her, by her presence, to bring peace and serenity wherever she found herself. Her choice of being obedient to the gospel engendered within, gestures of a vibrant faith, loving concern for others, generous availability to the will of God.

Many people came forth to give witness to the holiness of the life of Mother Bottego. Her cause for beatification has been introduced in Rome.

The reading of her life experiences and spiritual graces speak to us of the beauty of a life lived in conformity with Gospel values. Her life encourages us to open our hearts to that Grace which Mother Bottego so often wished for her daughters: "Oh if only we, my daughters, could hear those words addressed to Mary: 'Blessed are you because you have believed'."

I thank Fr. Maloney, who by this work, both repeats Mother's invitation and affords English speaking readers the possibility to come in contact with the priceless witness described in these rich pages.

Parma, 24 maggio 2002

Giuseppina Caccia
Directress general

CONTENTS

ACKNOWLEDGMENTS

I wish to express a word of sincere appreciation and gratitude to all who encouraged this work: Giuseppina Caccia, Superior General of the Missionaries of Mary and fourth successor of Mother Celestine Bottego who followed this endeavor closely and enabled it to happen.

Giovanna Meana, the Postulator of the cause for the beatification of Mother Bottego, was ever understanding, supportive, patient, and informative. Mirella Vergani the archivist, provided important documents. Anita Paganessi, the General Secretary of the Missionaries of Mary, was exact, tireless in reviewing the various efforts relative to this publication. Mariapia Gonzo, my able partner in the research in Butte, Montana, was a voice constantly insistent that this brief presentation should be completed.

Ellen Crain, Archivist of Silver Bow County, Butte, Montana provided a welcome and cooperation singular and most helpful. John Hughes, research librarian of the Butte Public Library provided his own expertise. Sister Dolores Brinkel, S.C.L., a local researcher, provided multiple legal documents regarding the Bottego family, their various properties, investments and their co-investors during their years in Butte.

In Ireland our research has not been completed but the assistance proffered by the Currid, Healy and Walsh families of County Sligo, has been priceless indeed.

Fr. Virginio Pugnoli, s.x. said it best: "Mother Bottego wished the Xaverians well always, and we are indebted to her for so very much." Fr. Augusto Luca, s.x. never ceased to offer contributions unlimited.

There are many Xaverians and others who deserve thanks. The list is endless. I here recall the names of all of the Missionaries of Mary, I have met and been touched by, and cannot but repeat as a refrain after each name, Mother's cherished expression:"Blessed are you, because you have believed!" Thank you!

INTRODUCTION

This is no biography. It has been an on-going chance discovery. In May 1995, while driving back to the east coast from California, I stopped briefly in Butte, Montana. The foundress of the Missionaries of Mary, Mother Celestine Healy-Bottego had lived there from 1896-1910.

After a few hours in the local library I found myself gazing at a house which may have been her home. I visited St. Patrick's Church where she had received first holy Communion and I obtained a copy of her Confirmation record from the parish office.

I met Mother Bottego in September 1954 when she first arrived in Petersham, Massachusetts to open the first residence of the Missionaries of Mary in America. We met again on a number of other occasions in San Lazzaro, Parma, Italy. I was acquainted with the dedicated work of her daughters in Asia, Latin America, Africa, Italy and here in America

In 1995, on the hundredth anniversary of her birth, Sr. Maria De Giorgi, a missionary sister working in Japan, wrote her biography entitled: "Va' e di' ai miei fratelli. Celestina Bottego, Fondatrice delle Missionarie Saveriane." The following pages draw heavily on that text, which I tried to complete, with previously little known information relative to her "American roots."

I returned to Butte and later visited Ironton, Cincinnati, Glendale in Ohio, County Sligo in Ireland, and San Lazzaro, Parma, Italy. Each place challenged me and produced missing pieces to my search. The story is far from being complete and further research is needed. It proved to be a journey of discovery. The following pages share something of the life of Mother Bottego. She was a singular person, who communicated faith, joy, love by word, eyes, example, heart and by her ever ready smile. She often declared: "Blessed are you because you have believed" – and that she did! [1]

Mother Bottego was born in Glendale, Ohio on December 20, 1895.
She lived in Butte, Montana from 1896-October 1910 when her mother and she joined other family members in Italy.
She founded the Missionaries of Mary on May 24, 1944 and she died on August 20, 1980 in Parma, Italy.
Her cause of beatification was opened first in Parma on April, 22, 1995 and then in Rome on January 12, 1998.

The Xaverian missionary congregation was founded in Parma, by Blessed Guido M. Conforti on December 3, 1895. He envisioned, but did not live to see the foundation of a sister missionary community since he died in 1931.

However 50 years later Fr. Giacomo Spagnolo s.x., became aware of Blessed Conforti's unfinished dream. He

[1] Mother Bottego often presented the Blessed Mother as the Model for the sisters. She wrote: "The most beautiful praise which was given to the Blessed Mother, I believe, are the words: 'Blessed are you, Mary, because you have believed'." (Aug. 25, 1968) Mother Bottego repeated those words often in her letters: "May Jesus bless you, and give you the light, strength and humility of the Blessed Mother. 'Blessed are you, Mary, because you have believed'." (Sept. 8, 1969) "I remember that when we alone had to decide our future after having abandoned the hospital of Kiliba, I found great strength when I thought of Our Blessed Mother and repeated: 'Blessed are you, Mary, because you have believed'." (Apr. 21, 1970) "Our missionary life is all an act of faith. 'Blessed are you, Mary, because you have believed'." (Apr. 2, 1970)

invited Celestine Bottego to help the dream be realized. She doubted in her ability and pondered the matter over in her heart. Fr. Spagnolo subtly approached her with a 1944 Easter greeting and holy card image of a crucifix with only the word "tutto/all"[2] inscribed on it. That gesture triggered a reply which was simple, spontaneous, and decisive: *"Ecce ancilla Domini (behold the handmaid of the Lord), God help me to be generous and perseverant in my resolutions."*[3] The Missionaries of Mary were born. Both communities, the Xaverian missionaries and the Missionaries of Mary, share common inspirations, mission goals, like ideals.

Mother Bottego, on the day of decision, May 24, 1944, was 48 years old. She was American by birth, Irish-American by temperament, Italy was her home. She was a Lady!

"Come, follow me!" The Lord whispered to her - she did just that throughout her life in Montana, Parma, India, Massachusetts, Brazil, Congo, Burundi, and beyond. The rest is history. Celestine Bottego, born in the new world, was a foundress of a religious community in the old world, and missionary to the whole world.

Robert S. Maloney, s.x.

[2] "Tutto" means "all." This word reminds us that Jesus gave his "all" for us. This word is an invitation to give our "all" to Jesus who poured out His life for us on the cross.

[3] "Behold I am the handmaid of the Lord." (Lk 2,38)

I

TALE OF AN EXTRAORDINARY FAMILY

1. Family origins – Italy

Agostino Bottego was a doctor in the town of Praticello, Reggio Emilia, in northern Italy. He lived there with his wife Maria Accinelli Bottego and their three children, Celestina, Gian Battista and Vittorio. The unification of Italy was evolving. Victor Emmanuel II was proclaimed King of Italy on March 17, 1861. Doctor Bottego decided to relocate his family in a rich farm area near the city of Parma in northern Italy. He purchased a house and ample farmlands in San Lazzaro, a suburb on the outskirts of the city of Parma.

Celestina, his daughter, married in 1881 and moved to Sicily. His two sons, Gian Battista and Vittorio, were sent to better schools. The boys were much alike in many ways. Both were adventurous, inquisitive, and each was gifted with a youthful vibrant spirit. Vittorio followed a military career and in 1887 he volunteered for service in Libya. Africa captured his imagination. Upon the completion of his military service, he opted to return to East Africa and carry out explorations under the auspices of the Italian Geographical Society. His explorations won him singular recognition and meritorious place in geographical circles in Europe.

Gian Battista, the elder son, was impatient with his studies. His innate creativity prodded him to investigate the new in the fast changing world around him. Agostino, his father, concerned that his son was not settling down, offered him three hundred lire and the possibility to move out to find himself. Gian Battista took the offer. He set out for France, and then continued on to America. The year was 1880. He was twenty-two.

Gian Battista (John B. in America) initially settled in Chester, Pennsylvania where he was employed as a metal worker, making steel for railroad tracks. In a letter to his parents he described himself as "dirty, half naked, sweaty," from his work at the smelters.[1] On the weekends during the summer, he was a hawker on the boardwalk

3

of Atlantic City where he peddled Italian leather gloves, which he received from his parents. He was a survivor. In 1882 he traveled from Chester to New Mexico, then on to California mining camps and finally to Butte, Montana in 1890. He was a man of initiatives, and he became a person with connections in Butte.

2. Family origins – Ireland

In Ballinafad, Sligo County, near Lough Arrow in the foothills of Mt Curlew there is an old Healy family homestead.[2] The Healy families in the area are and were many. In the early nineteenth century the penal laws[3] weighed heavily on local Catholic farmers. Bartholomew, the eldest son of one of these families, was sent to Boston. He was to pioneer the way and earn money for the forty-five day ocean crossing in steerage for his ten brothers and his fiancée. The new world beckoned and it seemed to offer great opportunities.

Bartholomew Healy[4] initially settled in Boston. In 1848 during the "potato famine" period in Ireland[5] Johanna Nally, his bride to be, joined him there. Bartholomew and Johanna married around 1850[6] and they then moved to Ohio where three children were born. Thomas, the eldest, died as a child soldier in the Civil War.[7] James set out on his own at an early age and settled in California during the later years of the gold rush. Mary was born on September 20, 1854, in one of Ironton's poor iron workers' huts along the shore of the majestic Ohio river.[8] Mary was orphaned by her mother's death before 1857.

Bartholomew then married Margaret McGovern[9] and settled in Cincinnati where two additional children, Thomas and Mark[10] were born. The Healy family later moved to Glendale, Ohio[11] where Margaret died at the good Samaritan hospital in 1873.

Bartholomew Healy had left Ireland for a land unknown, with no hope to return. He was only a simple, hard-working country boy who could neither read nor write. His was the common lot for many Irish children, namely, to pioneer and trail-blaze a path in America for other family members to follow. He had learned the iron trade in Ironton, Ohio, and later was employed as a metal worker in Cincinnati. His dreams and wanderlust eventually brought him to join his son, James, a novice gold miner, in California. From there he returned to Glendale, Ohio, where he died.

3. The Healy-Bottego family in Montana

John Bottego, son of Agostino Bottego, and Mary the daughter of Bartholomew Healy, met in northern California initially.

In 1891 John Bottego left California alone for Butte, Montana with the dream of earning $50,000 in two years. He did not reach his goal but he did earn $15.00 a day, a very substantial salary for that time. Mary Healy joined him by the end of the following year and they established their home there. Their first child, Maria (Marietta), was born in Butte a year later.

Montana [12] was a territory which was opened up to settlers after the Lewis and Clark expedition in April 1805. It remained a territory until 1864, until it became a state on November 8, 1889. Montana is called "sky country," for its natural beauty and the majestic verdant forested mountains which tower over and encircled this frontier city located along the continental divide in the Rockies.

The city of Butte took its name from its geographical shape. A butte was an isolated hill, rich in minerals, with steep or precipitous sides. Placer gold had been discovered there in 1864 and $1,500,000 of gold had been mined by 1869. Silver was first successfully treated there in 1875 but its production in Butte declined markedly after a price drop in 1893. Butte was primarily "a copper camp." By 1900 copper mining in Butte produced 50% of the national output of that metal. The railroad had reached Butte in 1880, and this along with the discovery of new mining fields accelerated the growth of this important frontier city.

Butte was an immigrant city with a polyglot population.[13] In nineteenth century America, cultural differences and boundaries disappeared gradually but slowly. Butte, however, was a mining city and workers often fell victim to mine related accidents and illnesses.[14] As a result, neighborhood cultural barriers in Butte were more easily crossed. People were people, and neighbors were neighbors.

It is said that the Butte City Hall clock never kept the right time. Why should it in a place where residents told time by the mine whistles?[15] In the hustle and bustle of frontier life and mining camps money came easy and more easily was it squandered. In Butte the interests of the early copper barons met face-to-face later with union concerns. "Lock out" came to mean "can do," in neighborhoods which mirrored ethnic pride. Butte, Montana, made a lasting impression on those who come in contact with its history. It is and has been one of the most unique, colorful, historic towns in America.[16] Families from many and varied lands came to Butte seeking success. Too frequently they found illness, challenges, and shattered hopes instead. As the mines multiplied, the rich amassed fortunes while the plight of the miners was struggled. Miners were courageous, daring, hard working, god fearing as is evidenced by the words inscribed on the monument memorial erected to honor victims of the Spectator mine disaster in Butte on June 8, 1917.[17]

The head frames of the mine shafts were called "gallows," because of their shape. Perhaps the "gallows" served as reminders that mining was a dangerous calling, and many were the men who lost their lives thousands of feet below the surface.[18] In 1999 the Montana

State Legislature allotted a substantial sum of money to preserve ten "gallow" mine head frames in Butte.[19] They stand as monuments to a suffered, dedicated, proud and unforgettable past. In years passed Christmas was celebrated as a special time of year in the mining camps. The joy of the season momentarily overcame the drab sameness of the mines. The "gallows" mine frames were illumined with multicolored lights recalling the tale of Christ's birth and christian hope[20] in the midst of human travail.

The 1889-1906 period in Butte was referred to as the "age of the Copper barons."[21] On August 12, 1897, William Jennings Bryant, candidate for the presidency of the United States visited Butte. President T. Roosevelt visited on May 29, 1903, and President Taft went to Butte in September 1909.

The church in Butte was missionary. Indian affairs on the western slope of the Rockies were followed and directed by the Belgian Jesuit missionary, Pierre Jean De Smet, S.J. (1801-1873). St. Patrick's parish, the first church in Butte, was dedicated in 1879. The first resident pastor, Fr. John Dols, a Belgian arrived in Butte on March 8, 1881.[22] The present St. Patrick's, frequented by the Bottego family during their years there, was dedicated on September 17, 1884. Mons. Peter de Siere, was the pastor of St. Patrick's church from the spring of 1893 until August 1918. In that year Fr. Joseph Venus, a Wisconsin native, was appointed its first American born pastor.[23]

The Bottego family had been living in Butte only three years when Mary's father, Bartholomew Healy, became seriously ill. In the autumn of 1895 Mary H.[24] Bottego decided to travel to Glendale, Ohio to visit her father. Mary was accompanied on the trip by her two-year-old daughter, Maria, and she was expecting her second child. The train ride was 2133 miles long. At that time passenger trains were comfortable enough but a trip that long was quite tiresome and tedious.[25] Glendale, Ohio, was a small, well-designed suburb a few miles to the north of Cincinnati. Mary had left there in 1873 after her stepmother's death. She never forgot the flowers, gardens and quaintness of Glendale throughout her years in distant Montana. During this 1895 visit with her father she was able to meet old friends and reminisce about her own early childhood days and schooling in Ohio.

Mary's father, Bartholomew Healy, died on October 28, 1895. He was laid to rest in the now extinct Holy Rood cemetery on the next day. The death of a parent or family member is a time of loss, remembrance, closure and an occasion to recall happier times. James, her brother who had settled in upstate Ohio, would have been present. Thomas, their brother, who had been killed in the Civil War before his fifteenth birthday, was absent, missed and remembered. She may have encountered her half-brothers, Thomas and Mark, of whom she retained fond remembrances. Once her father died, Mary's own ties with Glendale were severed forever. She was an expectant mother. Her concerns were now centered on her own family, her daughter and child about to be born.

4. Celestine Bottego was born in Glendale, Ohio

Celestine Bottego was born on Friday, the twentieth of December 1895 in Glendale, Ohio. John B. Bottego had remained in Butte because of his work. When he heard of the birth of Celestine, he wrote to his wife: *"I am happy to learn of the birth of our child. I feared that you might have a difficult time. Everything went well. We now have two little girls. I would not trade them in for anything else. I imagine how happy Maria (Marietta) must be. She is so expansive, enthusiastic, innocent. She has a good heart, spontaneity of spirit, and a determined will. I trust that both children will grow well, and find happiness in life. Their happiness depends greatly on all that their moth-*

8

er imparted to them before birth. A good education has a part to play. Stay well, be serene, and happy." [26]

Celestine was baptized in St. Gabriel's Church, on Sunday, January 19, 1896 by the pastor, Rev. Nicholas Kelly. A new church has since replaced the original church built in 1859. The first church later served as a convent for the Sisters of Charity who staffed the local Catholic school. What remained of that original St. Gabriel's has since been incorporated into the present parish center.

The life of Celestine Bottego has roots then in America, Italy and Ireland. In the United States her family story follows a winding trail from Massachusetts and New York, and to Ohio and California's gold mines to the then "richest hill on earth" Butte, Montana.

Mary H. Bottego and her two young children were unable to return to Butte immediately. The winters are harsh in the central and northwestern states. She remained in Glendale until March 1896. During which time she was in touch with her own past. From neighbors and friends she became more acquainted about her father's world and life in Glendale.

On the trip homeward the train passed through fast growing cities and across plains once populated by native Americans. The battle of the Little Big Horn, where General Custer was defeated in 1879, had taken place in Montana. A decade earlier, on May 10, 1869, the transcontinental railroad opened the way to the west. Chinese railroad workers, who had labored to build the western section of the railroad, were now scattered in squalid ghettoes in frontier towns and rail cities like Butte. The train traveled across mountainous routes and Mary could well appreciate the natural and unique beauty of each state along the way. The voyage was a learning experience, but her children were small and they kept her busy.

Mary H. Bottego had set out from Glendale, Ohio which resembled a formal English garden, with well-chosen trees, greenery and colorful flower beds. It was a safe haven. She was returning to Butte which presented quite a contrast. Her Montana hometown was dusty, hot, rowdy, and its air was laced with heavy smog. Mary and her children arrived home in early spring. Since the family was now larger, more ample quarters had soon to be found.

By 1897 the Bottego family had settled in the "Travona addition" section of Butte, also known as "Sleepy Hollow." This part of the city was a collection of small residential and industrial buildings on the lower west side of Butte.[27] To the north was the "Hub Section" where there was a mixture of working class folks living amidst the homes of the wealthy. Initially the "Hub" was an Irish stronghold, a mining area. It was said that at night a person could hear ore trains passing through mine tunnels under the houses there.[28]

Mary and John Bottego owned a brick house and other property in the Travona addition. On November 3, 1897,[29] they made a down payment on a fairly good sized house on South Montana Street which became their family home.[30] The final payment on the house was made on May 6, 1903.

In Butte John Bottego had many irons in the fire. He was forty three years old and in the prime of his life.[31] He was a successful mining worker,[32] and had been a foreman at the Cora mine and later worked at the Belmont mines.[33] He was employed by Mr. Augustus Heinze, one of the "copper barons" of Butte.

John also worked as a leasor, and this work put him in business contacts with Mr. William A. Clark, also an influential and wealthy "copper baron."

John had built a number of smaller houses in Walkerville near the Cora mine which were rented or later sold outright to mine workers.[34]

John Bottego had invested in small mining initiatives, as did Mary since 1894.[35] Both John and Mary bought, sold, exchanged lands and properties, to increase and en-

10

hance real estate holdings near their home in the south-western part of the city. John became an American citizen on October 10th, 1896. A third child, Vittorio, was born on Friday, May 26, 1897.[36] The family was established and doing quite well in Butte. Things were looking up.

5. Vittorio Bottego, the explorer, died in Africa

In 1897 John Bottego learned that his younger brother, Vittorio, had been killed in East Africa during a geographic expedition on March 17,1897. On the eve of his final departure for Africa, Vittorio had written to his parents: *"I know that you're saddened by my leaving, but I can delay no longer. It is better for me to take a risk and accomplish something than to idly stand still and barely exist as a tree standing motionless by the side of the road."*[37]

John had written to his brother five years earlier: *"Vittorio, if you decide to leave military service, fear not. You will be successful in whatever you decide to do. However, I must be honest and express my feelings. Your desire to travel and seek glory and fame in a distant land seems strange and unreal. I believe you would agree with me if you would take some time and reconsider your decision."*[38]

John Bottego was profoundly shocked and shaken by his brother Vittorio's death. He thought of his aging parents alone in Parma. His only sister, Celestina, was living in distant Sicily. The vast farm lands needed a strong and helping hand. However, he was busy providing for his own family.

The Bottego brothers, John and Vittorio, had left home to discover new lands, explore the world on different continents, and seek new possibilities and find themselves in the process. Their departure from home did not, however, preclude a family reunion for them one day, but the return which circumstances now dictated, was totally unexpected. The story was not new. The

11

Healy brothers had also left their family homestead in Ireland in the 1840s. However, their farewell was final, their hope to return slim. John Bottego, obsessed with childhood memories and his strong Bottego family ties felt called homeward. Anguish and filial concerns over this pressing family necessity continued to torment John and his wife, Mary, for three long years until the year 1900.

Mary H. Bottego was familiar with the immigrant odyssey, she had lived it during her own earlier transient years in Ironton, Cincinnati and Glendale, Ohio.[39] Thomas' life was snuffed out by war, James tried his fortune in the elusive mining camps of distant California. Thomas and Mark, her half brothers, remained her charge in Glendale until 1873, when their mother died and they then had to fend for themselves. Mary was then free to set out on her own. She too traveled to the mining camps in northern California, visited friends in San Angelo Texas in 1885,[40] vacationed in Salt Lake City in 1890. She had met initially and known John Bottego in California, and joined him in Butte later where she had hoped to find stability. That chance 1897 newspaper clipping caused her new concerns and the future plight of her family was now insecure.

The American landscape was well sowed with pilgrim beginnings, and immigrant hopes. However, the hope laced "American dream" was often shattered for varied reasons by dark storm clouds even in the land of so-called promise.

John Bottego and the Healy family, before him, had known and encountered difficult and decisive moments in America. Nonetheless, they moved forward sustained by their faith in the human spirit and their belief in a provident God. Whenever hopes were dashed, unknown paths untrodden opened up before them.

By the end of 1900 John Bottego was forty-two years old. A family decision was taken. John, seven year old Maria and three year old Vittorio would leave for Italy.

While Mary H. Bottego, who was forty-six years old, would remain in Butte to deal with ongoing legal matters, and manage their joint family landed holdings. Celestine, who was approaching school age, would remain as well.[41] It was a critical moment, and it marked the beginning of a decade long period of separation.

6. A decade long separation followed

How suffered and Irish-like was that family separation! It was difficult for the parents and for the children as well. All three of the Bottego children (Maria, Celestine and Vittorio) had earlier been enrolled in the local school system close to home in the area where the Webster public school was located. Five-year-old Celestine was no passive or stoic bystander in this family trauma. It was for her a sad moment. The trip across the American continent for her father and her siblings was long, the ocean voyage even longer. Letters provided some contact, but these letters were few and far between.

John Bottego's pioneering spirit, appreciation of things new, family values, sense of justice and goodness to neighbors, friends, workers were all part of the heritage which Celestine culled from her now absent father. During this period of separation, Mary H. Bottego and Celestine, mother and daughter, drew ever closer together.

When John Bottego left America,[42] his wife Mary was already deeply engaged in a very complex civil suit initiated in December of 1899.[43] She lost that case in December 1904 in the Montana Supreme Court. Justice was often blind and unjust on the frontier. Although she was American born, she was a woman, a person from out of state. She put her trust in the system and well-qualified advisers. The "cut throat mortgage" system, which was applied to a loan she had made, was a procedure later outlawed. Despite this financial setback, her losses were

13

minimal. She realized a substantial financial gain nonetheless on the property put up as collateral. Even though she was obliged to buy back that property for a higher price she was later able to sell it at a good profit. She was a shrewd and able administrator.

Mary H. Bottego made the education and religious training of Celestine, her daughter, a prime concern.[44] The Sisters of Charity of Leavenworth, Kansas had come to Butte to work in the hospital in 1881. They later worked in St Patrick's parish school which was opened in 1889.[45] Following the advice of a priest who had come to preach a parish mission, Mary H. Bottego transferred Celestine to St. Patrick's grammar school in 1902. Celestine received her first communion at St Patrick's church on June 3, 1906. She was confirmed there on May 5, 1907 by the Rt. Rev. John P. Carroll, Bishop of Helena, Montana.[46]

Mary H. Bottego was a woman of courage and determination. Travel was familiar to her. She prized her family ties with her brother James who, in his later years lived in Ohio, was often a visitor to Butte. Her heart was heavy though because of the separation from her husband and children. She kept her feelings to herself, however. The family and the good of the children came first. Mail became less frequent and communication became more difficult over the years, Maria (Marietta) had forgotten English and Celestine knew no Italian. Yet, when the reunion of the family occurred in 1910, it seems to have taken place with relative ease. The ten-year separation was over, it had been accepted as an unfortunate necessity, the future looked brighter. Few negative nuances regarding this long separation were evidenced.

Mary H. Bottego was a woman of faith. She had most probably been schooled in Ohio by the Sisters of Charity of Cincinnati. Knowledge and learning were high priorities for her. The Bottego home in San Lazzaro, Italy was known to be a place where neighbors turned in time of need. The Bottego home in Butte could not have been much different. Mary had experienced her share of hardship, family losses, uncertainty, new beginnings. She had been tooled and well informed about the Healy odyssey in America. As a result she instilled Celestine with an appreciation of Irish song, dance, story telling, and family origins. Her teaching was more by example than by words. Although she had been born in Ohio, Mary, nonetheless, possessed a good bit of Irish lore. She was hard working and valued religious moral guidance.

During this time Mary H. Bottego taught Celestine a favorite prayer of hers. *"Let nothing trouble you, nothing scare you – All is fleeting – God alone unchanging – Patience everything obtains – Who possesses God nothing wants – God alone suffices."* This was a prayer of St. Teresa of Avila.

Mary H. Bottego was an able caretaker of property, a defender of the rights of her family. She was an example of steadfastness, fidelity, faith, hope to her daughter and prize pupil, during their ten year exile from family together. Mary had not herself enjoyed a normal family life. She would have wanted her children to have what she did not have [47] but it was not to be.

Mary recognized and appreciated her own struggled personal story and worth. Her life journey had helped her focus. She knew who she was, where she had come from and where she was going. She was independent and self sufficient. She taught Celestine like values, serenity and joy, welcome and compassion, goodness and hope. She was the confidante of Celestine's vocation awareness in Butte, and she enabled Celestine to become a joyful young lady in Butte, and the young woman who won over the hearts of simple folk in San Lazzaro later. Mary H. Bottego was selfless. In Italy she would have to struggle with new culture, language, usages and she did so. She was a mother who risked much for the good of her children. She did not look back. Butte was merely another stage on her voyage, and the polluted air of the copper camp had not proved to be beneficial to her health. [48]

Celestine Bottego in later years described her time in Montana: *"It was a great grace to have lived close to my mother. She had a strong moral fiber, and a sweet disposition. Her heart was great, and her speech was seasoned with a profound sense of typical Irish humor. She spoke to me of serious matters as well.*

Together we read many wonderful books in English. She had me learn by heart the poems which she held dear. She tried her best to impart the best education possible. She encouraged me to study music, play the piano, learn to care for our home and about many other and useful things."

In August 1909, about a year before leaving for Italy, Mary H. Bottego borrowed travel money from the Butte-based Hanson-MacPherson Company.[49] The Bottego property on S. Montana was quite valuable. One home located on that property ended up on the auction block in 1920 because of a ten-year default in taxes.[50] Other Bottego owned lands there and elsewhere in the Travona addition were later sold for unpaid taxes as late as July 8, 1944 and September 21, 1957 unbeknown to the Bottego family in Italy.

The influence of her mother, the Sisters of Charity and the pastoral guidance of Mons. Peter de Siere, may have all contributed in fostering and nourishing a vocation in young Celestine. Mother Bottego many years later recalled: *"During a day of recollection in my last school year (1910), the confessor asked me if I had ever considered the religious life. I told him that I had to leave for Italy, but confessed that the thought of a religious vocation was "ever present." My mother had decided that we leave for Italy once I finished my studies."*[51] Celestine's "persistent" vocation, as a result, would have to wait for other times and other places, but it remained "persistent."

The final year of school for Celestine at St. Patrick's school ended.[52] The "Butte's Miner" newspaper on July 24, 1910 carried the photo of Celestine Bottego who was named the best grammar school student in the state of

Montana in that year. Celestine was justly proud and anxious to bring a copy of the newspaper to Italy to show to her father. Mary and Celestine Bottego traveled across America and stopped in various states where they visited distant Healy relatives and acquaintances from July until they left for Europe from New York on October 10, 1910.

Celestine was excited and no doubt enthusiastic over the ocean voyage. Mary, her mother, however, was leaving homestead, roots, hopes, and country. She was now fifty-six years old, endowed with memories of events, people, places. Mary H. Bottego faced a new chapter of her life. Her desire to have the family again united alone made her trip less difficult and her future choices easier.

Tucked away in Celestine's luggage were a few photographs of things and people held dear. There was a photo of St. Patrick's Church, the certificate of her first Communion, photos of acquaintances, and her newspaper nomination as best grammar student in the state of Montana in 1910.

In Italy Mary H. Bottego and Celestine were expected, long awaited, and most welcome at the home of the Maria Accinelli Bottego, the widow of the late Agostino Bottego, where John B. Bottego, Maria (Marietta), and Vittorio were living. Butte, the gallows mine frames, the mines, mountains, paved and unpaved hilly streets, the neighbors from many nations and cultures, the native Americans, the Chinese railroad workers and miners were all memories left behind. Their Bottego home in San Lazzaro was located at the end of the tree lined earth paved entrance road. The farm lands were spacious, and in the different seasons fields were filled with crops of many types. There was much to talk about, a new language, new customs to learn and new acquaintances to make. Maria (Marietta) and Vittorio possessed little English and Celestine now had to study Italian.

There were news family roots to discover. Butte had profoundly marked the first fifteen years of Celestine's life. She had heard about Italian art, music, culture, now she had occasion to learn much about her Italian roots. Celestine cherished her American sojourn with her mother and treasured the Irish faith and cultural values which her mother had instilled in her during the long months and years which they shared on S. Montana Street. The Lord had been the guide of Celestine's journey. Her vocation call remained, even though it had been placed on a back burner, until a future right moment. One moment of her life had closed, another opened up before her. Each page bore witness to her life focused interiorly on the Lord, externally on the needs of others. The lofty mountains of the continental divided uniquely proclaimed God's presence, and the faces of Butte's diverse humanity invited neighborly compassion and concern. The Apennines in Italy now embraced her as did the simple folk of San Lazzaro.

Notes:

[1] Letter of John Bottego to his father from Chester, Pennsylvania 1882.

[2] Sligo 693 sq.mi., 1795 sq.km. An area of small farms (10-12 acre in size) where animals are raised and crops cultivated. The eastern boundaries stretch across plateaux; the southwest boundary passes across a varied countryside to Lough Arrow. It rises to cross the Curlew mountains, an altitude of 828 ft, and runs over small farms. In 1956 there were 56,850 people in Co. Sligo, and in 1961 it was 51,558. There is a 62.3% density of the population per sq.mi.

[3] The oral history transmitted by the Healy family in America give the "penal laws" as a reason for the emigration of Bartholomew Healy who was born in 1820. It may well be surmised that Bartholomew came to America because of failing crops in the pre-famine and potato famine years.

[4] The family was known in Ireland as Healy. When members of the family arrived in Boston, it would seem that they were listed in local city directories as "Haley." In Ohio both spelling, Healy and Haley, were used by the ancestors of Mother Bottego. Mary H. Bottego always used "Healy" as her maiden name during her years in Montana. Family names were quite often altered when immigrants arrived in America.

18

[5] In 1847, two years after the potato blight destroyed the crop on which the Irish poor relied, almost 106,000 Irish immigrated to the United States. In the next seven years, 1848-1854, 1.1 million more left Ireland... famine immigrants were 40% of the whole American Immigration for those years. They came to a nation unprepared for massive infusions of people, particularly people poor beyond the normal powers of description and embracing a religion and culture different from what the host society knew and clearly preferred. Emigrant pushes are always selective, and the famine selected those Irish least equipped to handle the demands of the industrialized American cities they entered. They were typically rural, Catholic, Irish speaking, unskilled, tied to family and community, and impoverished. The Famine immigrants had little in the way of advance Irish presence, few established Irish communities to contain and comfort them. These Irish Americans had to construct a world on hostile ground with scant resources. "The Butte Irish, Class and ethnicity in an American Mining Town 1875-1925" by David Emmons, University of Illinois Press 1990, pg. 1.

[6] Johanna Nalley arrived in Boston from Cork in steerage on the "M. D. Chase" on October 9, 1848. The crossing took forty five days.

[7] Thomas was killed in the Civil War on the Union side. He was young, born in Ohio between 1850-1853. 77,844 troops from Ohio enlisted in the Union forces by December 31, 1861. Cincinnati was threatened by Confederate forces in September 1862. Confederate forces under Morgan carried out raids in Ohio in 1863. Hamilton county was a battleground. Thomas may well have been picked up as a local boy to fight in area skirmishes, or he may have enlisted in the Union army in another state. No record of his service, pension application, or death has been found. The Healy family oral history speaks of his military service and death. Between April 1861-April 1865 240,514 Ohio enlistments (many were 2nd and 3rd enlistments for a given period) were recorded.

[8] Mary Healy was born on Wednesday, September 20, 1854 and was baptized on Thursday October 5th in St Lawrence O'Toole church, Ironton. The sponsors were Michael Gardiner and Honora Healy. Honora, wife of Patrick, resident of Ironton, may have been related to Bartholomew. Michael Gardiner was a next door neighbor of the Ironton Healys. Bartholomew may have remained in Ironton briefly to learn something of the iron trade. From 1859-1862 he worked in Cincinnati making iron grates and mantles. Ironton, the most southernmost point of Ohio, was founded in 1849, in the heart of the hanging rock region of Lawrence county. In the 1850 census Ironton and a number of other towns were grouped together as "Upper." Ironton was once the largest center of pig iron production in the world. As a terminal of the Iron Railroad and as a shipping port on the Ohio river, Ironton grew rapidly, becoming the county seat of Lawrence County in 1851. On September 3, 1850 the census population of "Upper,"

including Ironton, had 417 residences, 425 families, 1344 white men, 1142 white women, 5 colored men and 3 colored women, total of 1349 males, and 1145 women.

[9] Bartholomew Haley married Margaret McGovern on Wednesday December 7th, 1857 at St Francis Xavier church, Fr. Charles Driscoll S.J. (a native of Belgium) officiated. St Francis Xavier church served as Cathedral of Cincinnati from 1822-1845. Margaret McGovern Haley died on June 6, 1873, in Good Samaritan hospital, and was buried in the Holy Rood Catholic cemetery in Glendale, Ohio.

[10] Thomas, a son of the second marriage, was born on January 23, 1859, Mark was born on October 8, 1860, in Cincinnati, Ohio. Bartholomew Haley's eldest child in his first marriage was Thomas also. The repetition of the name might indicate that the two boys on the first marriage may have been living with relatives elsewhere.

[11] Glendale, Ohio, originated in 1851 and incorporated in 1855, was a residential development for directors of the Proctor & Gamble Co. and railroad executives. Glendale remains one of the earliest planned community in Ohio, if not in the United States. It is a National historic landmark. Glendale's population is 2,188 (in 2000) and contains 946 residential homes within 1,012 acres (1.67 square miles) of densely wooded parcels fronting curvilineal streets that are lined with original gas lights. More than 392 acres of Glendale incorporate a unique historic district and are home to 59 of the pivotal structures from the 1850s.

[12] Not the least of Butte's resources is its remarkable history. One of America's most intriguing melting pots, most bizarre corporate battlegrounds, and most interesting historic places, the city savors its past and works increasingly to preserve it. History, however, is more than antiquarian reminiscences of colorful mining kings and epic doings of yesteryear. Much more weightily, history is the burden of attitudes, mores, prejudices, loves and hatreds rooted in the economic, social and political milieu which formed over a hundred years ago. Thus the battle for Butte, which ended seventy five years ago, has colored much of Montana's subsequent history. The battle for Butte was a rich slice of Americana, a classic instance of raw, unrestrained frontier capitalism. It brought great wealth to a handful of willful men, gave employment to thousands more, and brought a quick and peculiar form of industrialization to a remote corner of the mountain west. It corrupted the political culture of an American state and shocked the sensibilities of a nation which took three generations to dissipate. Like the frontier, Butte was rich, unabashedly exploited, turbulent and endlessly fascinating. Michael P. Malone, "The Battle for Butte," Helena: Montana Historical Society Press, 1995, pg. 217.

[13] Butte's people were from Cornwall, England, Ireland, Norway, Sweden, Denmark, Serbia, Croatia, Austria, Slovenia, France, Germany, Switzerland, China. There were black Americans, native Amer-

icans and in later times there were Italians, Jews, Greeks, Lebanese, Spaniards and Mexicans. See Pat Kearney, pg. 133ff.

[14] Butte mines were the most unsafe hard rock operations in the world. Accidental deaths occurred on a monthly basis with over 2,100 workers losing their lives underground during the duration of mining operations in Butte... People always talk about the deaths in the Butte mines. Few realize that all the accidents in the mines kept the hospitals as busy as the undertakers. There were wards full of miners in the hospital all the time with broken legs, ankles, backs, arms and other things from working underground. It was a very unsafe profession especially in Butte. They had something once a week in the emergency room of the hospital called "miners' hours." It was during that time that miners could come in and receive medical attention from local doctors for cuts, bruises and other injuries suffered on the job. If workers were not being hurt or killed in the mines, they were certain to be dying a slow death through breathing the dirty air underground. From 1894-1901 Montana miners suffered a fatality rate of 3.53 per 1000, higher than Colorado, Idaho, South Dakota, Britain and Germany. Kearney, pg. 16-18.

[15] Copper Camp, pg. 4.

[16] This hill, once called the richest on earth, is known now as one of the dirtiest sites in America. Its soils and waters are filled with lead and other toxic metals, and the creek called Silver Bow, which flows at its base, was until recently so contaminated by runoff that it was poisoned at least 140 miles downstream. Butte is a "National Historic Landmark" and today it is the largest site of a cleanup program for toxic waste in the world. See. William Langewiesche "The Profits of Doom" in the Atlantic Monthly, April 2001, pg. 56-62 and Kearney, the forward.

[17] J.D. Moore wrote his wife: "This may be the last message you will get from me. If anything happens to me you had better sell the house...go to California...know your Jim died like a man, his last thoughts were for his wife that I love better than anyone on earth. We will meet again. Tell mother and the boys goodbye." And later: "My dear little wife, try not to worry. I know you will but trust in God, everything will come out all right."

Manus Duggan wrote to his wife: "Have not confided my fears to anyone but have looked and looked for hope but if the worst comes I myself have no fears but welcome death with open arms, as it is the last act we all must pass through – and all is natural – it is God's will – we should have no objection." "It breaks my heart to be taken from you so suddenly and unexpectedly but think not of me, for if death comes, it will be in sleep without suffering, I ask pardon for any suffering I have ever caused." The Spectator mine produced 2000 lbs of ore from 2000 feet. 410 men were down to 2400 feet when the fire broke out. 167 miners were killed in that tragic accident on June 8th, 1917.

[18] See Kearney, pg. 16ff. "The story of mine disasters and fires were a major component of life in Butte. The fear of accidents and death Butte mining families had to endure every day. I lost my father in the mines when I was sixteen years old. It was a real shock and it took a long time to get over." "As a child I used to watch my dad go off to work every day. One day he never came home. He was killed in an accident in the West Colusa mine." "I remember a guy working in the Belmont mine got his leg cut up real bad when it got caught in the tracks." "Only few mines on the hill had any type of ventilation. The average life span of a Butte miner was 45 years." Pgs. 16ff. At the beginning of the century (1900) Butte boasted that its copper mines had yielded almost two billion dollars, and in the same breath admitted that it was the only Western city whose cemetery population exceeded that of its living residents. "Copper Camp", pg. 8.

[19] See "County gets head frame preservation money" in The Butte Weekly, Vol. 2, No 50 – July 14, 1999.

These are black steel elevator derricks, called gallow frames which dominate the city skyline. From these miners were lowered as much as a mile into the labyrinth of mine corridors below.

[20] "I was sitting in the day room in Ondal, India, during my World War II days. Someone turned on the phonograph and from the speaker came the voice of Deanna Durban singing, 'I can see the lights of home.' As I listened my thoughts drifted ten thousand miles away to the top of Harding way and my eyes became filled with tears, as I remembered the bright lights of Butte from that vantage point." See Kearney, the forward.

[21] The hill on which Butte was built contains 7,000 miles of wood framed horizontal tunnels. There were 40 miles of vertical shafts to access the underground mine areas. In 1891 the average wage of the 4800 men working in the mines of Butte was $100 a month or $3.50 a day. Horses and mules were primary fixtures in Butte's underground mines. It is estimated that 1,000 mules worked at one time underground. Prior to 1910 over 10,000 animals had worked in Butte's mines. Once below they only came back to sunlight if there was a long strike, or when they were too old to work. During the mining history of Butte there were some 220 mines functioning. Butte is the most heavily mined ground in the world. Kearney, pg. 36ff. and William Langewiesche, "The Profits of doom" in The Atlantic Monthly, April 2001 pg. 50-62.

[22] Butte was incorporated as a city in 1879. With the growth of population, the little mission of St Patrick's became a parish in its own right. The first pastor arrived by stagecoach from Deer Lodge on March 8, 1881. He was greeted by a small but enthusiastic group who proudly announced: "We're from St Patrick's." As he stepped down from the coach he affirmed, "I'm from St Patrick's too." See "St. Patrick's Parish 100 years 1881-1981."

[23] St. Patrick's church was built in 1881. The city was growing

rapidly. During the brief time that Celestine lived there the following churches were built: Sacred Heart in 1903, St. Mary's in the same year, Holy Savior in 1904, St. Joseph's in 1905, Immaculate Conception in 1907.

[24] Mary H. Bottego is the way that Celestine's mother referred to herself in Butte, Montana.

[25] "Nothing like it in the World," Stephen E. Ambrose: Simon and Schuster, New York, 2000. The transcontinental railroad was finished on May 10, 1869. The Central Pacific section was built by Chinese, the Union Pacific part by the Irish. Both groups faced discrimination, hiring signs read "dogs and Irish need not apply." Cf. pg 378. The Union Pacific Railroad built a spur line between Ogden, Utah and Butte, Montana by Christmas 1881. In 1869 a person could move across America at sixty miles an hour and go from New York to San Francisco in seven days. The cost was $150 for first class, $70 for emigrants. By June 1870 the price was only $136 for first class, $110 for second class and $65 for third class. First class meant a Pullman sleeping car, while emigrants sat on a bench, cf. pg. 369. John Bottego earned $15 a day in 1900.

The trip from Butte, Montana to Glendale, Ohio would have been about 2,133 miles (3,413 km). The route may have been Butte-Salt Lake City-Chicago-Cincinnati-Glendale. Senator Daniel Webster declared in 1947: "The railroad "towers above all other inventions of this or of the preceding age." Pg. 357. People of the second half of the nineteenth century "saw slavery abolished and electricity put to use, the development of the telephone and the completion of the telegraph, and most of all the railroad. The locomotive was the first great triumph over time and space. Once it came and after it crossed the continent of North America, nothing could ever be the same. It brought about the greatest change in the shortest period of time." Pg. 357.

[26] Maria De Giorgi, pg. 28.

[27] It got its name from the Travona Mine constructed there in 1876. A mixture of many different ethnic groups had settled in that area. The Serbians had enough people around the neighborhood to lead to the construction of the Holy Trinity Serbian Orthodox church on Idaho St. in 1905. In a two block radius around the Webster school there were ten different small grocery stores. The Washoe Sampling Center was located on the southern part of the Travona Addition close to the railroad tracks.

[28] Kearney, pg. 201-208.

[29] The grant deed for property described the lot and included the conditioning clause: "Excepting and reserving however, from this conveyance all ores and minerals beneath the surface of the above described premises, with the right to mine for and extract the same, provided that in the exercise of such mining right the surface thereof shall not be disturbed or interfered with or in anyway damaged."

[30] Reference is made to these properties in the documents of Mary

H. Bottego's court case (1899-1905), in letters between the family in Italy and in the United States.

[31] John initially lived alone at 405 N. Montana rear in 1891. When Maria was born in 1893 John and Mary Bottego were living at 102 W. Granite. They later moved to 464 E. Galena and later bought their home on S. Montana in 1897.

[32] John Bottego is listed in the city directories as a foreman in the Belmont mine until1899. In 1899 he was a "leasor" at the Cora mine. A "leasor" was a person who had a small group of miners working under him. The leaser and his crew scouted the area of the mines for new veins of ore. John did scout and purchase small mining properties and group them together to make a worthwhile piece of mining land for mining developers.

[33] The Belmont mine operated from 1900-1956. It was one of the hotter mines, shunned by miners from northern climates but attractive to mucker men (laborers who hand shoveled ore). Tons of red ore were hauled out through this nearly 70 year old head frame, which originally stood at the Cora mine where John Bottego had also worked. The Belmont mine was 3700 feet deep. See Kearney pgs. 36-42.

[34] Mary H. Bottego sold a three room frame house at the Cora Mining Claim to B. Roletto for $250.00. This was one of three such houses owned by the Bottego family in that place and time. Sale indenture dated December 2nd, 1902. In a letter, dated February 24, 1902, Mary H. Bottego wrote to her husband: "The houses at the Cora have not rented well... I should like to sell some property and clear the rest."

[35] Mary and John engaged in small mining investments, and in buying and selling of property. The deeds and documents bear one, or other, or both names. The house on S. Montana St. was initially bought in both names, but the 1903 the final deed bears Mary's name alone.

[36] Vittorio, son of John and Mary Bottego, was baptized in St Patrick's Parish on November 30, 1898 by Fr. Callaghan, the sponsor was Mrs. Sullivan. Fr. Callaghan was considered to be a real man of God, ready to help all. He died at the age of thirty-eight. Some 11,000 people, from, Butte, Helena, Anaconda, attended his funeral. "Copper Camp", pg. 190.

[37] Vittorio made two geographic trips to E. Africa. He discovered the sources of the Giuba River in Somalia, the course of the Omo River to Lake Rodolfo in Uganda, the upper course of the River Sobat, which flows from the right branch of the Nile. He was killed during these exploratory voyages on March 17, 1897.

[38] Letter of John Bottego, written from Chester, Pennsylvania on June 12, 1882 to his brother Vittorio in Italy. Maria De Giorgi, pg. 22.

[39] See John Clubbe " Cincinnati Observed" (Cincinnati: Ohio State University, 1992). Early settlers set off from Pittsburgh on flatboats

that drifted down stream at $3^1/_2$ miles an hour. The flatboats were of varying sizes and shapes, from twenty to one hundred feet in length, twelve to twenty feet wide. Of simple often shoddy construction, flat bottomed and square at the ends, they were managed by a single large oar and were barely water tight enough for a single voyage. Settlers arriving at their destination either broke up the boats to build their first cabins or sold them for lumber. Others poled rafts down the current. On board was the family cow, chickens, grandma's rocking chair and the baby in the cradle. "Hi-o, away we go, floating down the O-hi-o" sang thousands of immigrants. Flatboats, even rafts were still to be sighted along the Ohio as late as 1870. We may even consider the flatboats ancestors of the barges we find on the river today, pg. 166. The thing we remember most vividly is often the city we see first. The first view of Cincinnati most early settlers and travelers had was from the Ohio River. After floating hundreds of miles through often pristine forest, they rounded the bend at Mount Adams and there it was, a bustling metropolis in the midst of apparent wilderness. The experience never fails to amaze, pg. 158. The Ohio flows for 981 miles from Pittsburgh to Cairo Ill, but it also flows from century to century. Like the city before which it passes, the river represents a continuum, related both to past and future. For most of the nineteenth century, and to a greater degree than we may realize in the twentieth, the Ohio was – and remains – Cincinnati's artery of life, pg. 161.

[40] Mary Healy received a Christmas gift, a book entitled "Lucile," from a friend who signed the book K.C.S.

[41] Maria, Celestine, and Vittorio (he appeared as Hector in the school listings) were enrolled in the local school district. The Webster school has been built in 1897 at the corner of Idaho and Aluminum streets.

[42] John Bottego was in Italy in 1901. This date is contained in a sworn written statement (dated Dec. 3rd, 1901) made to the District Court of the Second judicial District of the State of Montana.

[43] Mary H. Bottego had taken out a loan for the purchase of additional property. She had placed a prime piece of property as collateral for the loan. John Bottego, perhaps concerned about his trip to Europe, did not pay the interest and capital due on this loan. The lending party employed the questionable practice of "a cut throat mortgage." The land placed as collateral was sold at public auction with a minimal newspaper notice being given. While the common practice of the time granted a grace period – during which the borrower whose "collateral property" (placed as a guarantee for the loan entered into) – was permitted to repurchase the "collateral property" by paying a minor fee or fine over and above the real value of the property. When the "cut throat" mortgage procedure was employed the "collateral property" was sold to the highest bidder and had to be repurchased at that excessive price. Mary Bottego was persistent and she fought in vain for rightful redress for five years.

25

[44] Maria De Giorgi, pg. 30.

[45] The Sisters of Charity of St. Elizabeth Seton were founded in 1809. The Sisters of Charity of Cincinnati were an offshoot of that earlier foundation in 1856.The Sisters of Charity of Nazareth, Kentucky were founded in 1812 by Catherine Spaulding and they followed the rule of Mother Seton. The Sisters of Charity of Leavenworth, founded in 1858 in Leavenworth, Kansas, were a branch of the Charity Sisters of Nazareth, Ky. They operated the Catholic Hospital in Butte from 1881, and began to teach in St Patrick's school in 1889.

[46] Mother Bottego recalled her first Communion years later with the words: "I am happy that you are preparing children for their first Communion. I know from my own experience (in America) how well this preparation was carried out. It left an indelible mark on me." (A letter of Mother Bottego dated April 26, 1967)

[47] On February 24, 1902 Mary H. Bottego wrote to her husband John: "Little Cell is growing to be a lovely girl and so bright at school. I think too much so for her years."

[48] In a letter, dated February 24, 1902, to her husband, John, Mary H. Bottego wrote: "I don't want to stay here. I have not been well this winter and a change will do me good."

[49] She arranged that the loan would be paid back by rent fees collected by the lending agency, as they came due on Bottego property in Butte. This financial arrangement was terminated, fully satisfied, paid, settled and discharged by the Bottego family from Italy on May 13, 1913. Radical changes in the economic climate of Butte at the time of the first world war lessened the income that the Bottego family might have expected.

[50] The house remained in the name of the Bottego family until 1920, when it was auctioned of by Silver Bow County for unpaid back taxes by the County of Silver Bow for about $2,000.

[51] Maria De Giorgi, pg. 30.

[52] From America Mother Bottego wrote to Fr. Spagnolo on October 1, 1954: "Perhaps I, more than others, have to see the examples given by those in religious life to correct myself and become more humble and gentle in dealing with souls. It was good for me to see that the impressions which I had of the Sisters who taught me when I was a child were true. In America religious sisters are well respected and thought of."

II

THE HEALY-BOTTEGO FAMILY REUNITED

1. Italy in 1910

The unification of Italy took place in 1870. The kingdom of Italy, however, continued to be divided by conflict between church and state, north and south, modern urban industry and semi feudal rural poverty. Parliamentary politics under the constitutional monarchy created a regime that was weak, and one which inspired little popular support.[53]

The Bottego family lived in San Lazzaro, a small rural suburb south east of Parma, which had once been an independent town. It was connected to the center of Parma by an old Roman road, the via Emilia. The name of the town "San Lazzaro" possibly derives from the word "Lazzaretto" which was a refuge or temporary hospice for travelers inflicted with a contagious disease.

The parish of San Lazzaro existed well before the year 1400. In 1802, Napoleon acquired the Duchy of Parma, and he taxed the citizenry, and church property. The verdant farm lands of the area had previously been drained, cultivated, reclaimed and used by Benedictine monks of the Abbey of San Giovanni in Parma. The fertile and rich lands of the monastery were later confiscated, and their ownership passed into other hands. The times demanded the separation of church and state, and church lands often enriched the local citizenry. Part of the extensive Bottego landed property had formerly been owned in the nineteenth century by the College of St Joseph in Parma or earlier by the Benedictine monks.[54]

During his years in Butte, Montana John Bottego had been a builder. He built small houses for miners working at the Cora mine, where he worked. That experience served John Bottego well in San Lazzaro where he embarked on an ambitious plan to provide housing for the farm workers living on his property. He also constructed a large multipurpose building on Via Casa Bianca in the center of San Lazzaro, called the "Palazzone," which was not far from the Bottego family home. This building served many. It was a local gathering point, a multi-purpose meeting place, and center for many activities for the local people.

Agostino Bottego, the father of John Bottego had died in 1909 and John, (or Battista as he was known in Italy), took over the management of the Bottego lands. John B. Bottego was not a difficult landlord. He was well respected, a good man ever ready to help out his farm hands and their dependents.

During the period 1901-1911 the socio-political climate in Italy and agriculture especially in the north, underwent greater changes than at any other time in its previous history. Irrigation schemes and improvements were pioneered by a new type of landowner, and by tenant farmers with large farms and long leases. The result was a more efficient "capitalist" type of agriculture. However, this period also produced a mass of laborers who could find work only at the busiest times of the year, as an "agricultural proletariat." There were grievances to be addressed. Many laborers had been evicted from lands they had long worked. The areas of advanced "capitalist" farming in northern Italy soon became centers of labor leagues, protracted strikes, and labor battles. Socialist trade unionism had enjoyed a rapid growth in 1901-1902. The aim of the socialist federations was to fight for higher wages. Socialism was in the air, the socialists often stepped in where Catholic organizers feared to tread. In 1911 only about one-fifth of the organized workers were in Catholic unions.[55]

Although Catholics were not deeply engaged in the political arena, the church in Italy spoke out strongly against modernism. Tension existed and mounted between the church and the state. Parma had experienced its first general strike in 1908 which lasted for fifty-seven days.

In the early part of the twentieth century textile workers, industrial laborers and others had been organized into a powerful work force in America. Unions were very

30

strong. The miners of Butte, Montana, who had experienced the tense struggle between the mine owners and themselves, were solidly engaged in the forefront of the ongoing fight for workers' rights.

Although Italy had fought with the Allied powers in World War I its meager gains acquired at the peace of Paris scarcely seemed to justify its wartime suffering and death toll of more than 600,000. In the post war period Europe was not peaceful. Totalitarianism and fascism were the current aggressive movements. Strikes multiplied, dissatisfaction spread, and even greater rifts appeared in public opinion which the war years had inadvertently shaped. The Russian revolution projected a certain degree of success. Riots ran rampant in Germany. Postwar economic dislocation, fear of communism, and political disillusionment abetted the rise of fascism. Diverse socialist groups were being drawn together. It was feared that a proletariat regime would take over in Italy. Parties on the left, and the right wing fascists clashed after the 1921 general elections, and during the 1922 strike. Benito Mussolini took over the Italian government at the invitation of the king in that year. The black shirt followers of Mussolini held their "March on Rome." The Provinces of Emilia, where Parma was located, and Romagna were not immune from these power struggle times. Party rivalries, power stratagems, played a role in establishing a new balance of power. Parma's socialists were openly anticlerical. The church and priests were singled out in negative and derogatory campaigns.

2. Celestine, discovering her new homeland

Celestine Bottego lived her early years in Italy in times marked by tension and power struggles. She was tactful and discreet. *"She showed no partiality. For her, people in need wore no distinctive garb or color, carried no special banner. Christian charity became her slogan and strategy."*[56] At school, in the parish, and among the family, Celestine was serene, available, generous, giving. Her characteristic traits, which had been acquired early, were deeply rooted, and provided her with strong interior motivation.

In Butte, neighbors were not strangers, they were "family." People spoke different dialects and languages, and carried different passports. Nationality diversity, social classes, life experiences found their place within a common humanity. Celestine lived amid Butte's neighborhood structures and she valued what she experienced there. She came to San Lazzaro with a unique sense of neighborliness. Celestine loved life. A photo from her days in Butte portrays a young lady filled with inner joy, serenity, peace and happiness. She was then almost fifteen years old. This spontaneity and friendship enabled her to make a quick and somewhat easier than expected transition from Butte to Parma, Italy, from a busy copper camp to the simple and rural lifestyle of San Lazzaro.

Celestine loved nature and the land. She appreciated the generous, determined, committed, qualities and simple, straightforward mannerisms of the farmers. She listened to the farm hands as they contested their low minimum wages. However, landholders, like her father, stuck to their positions and defended their right to hold to the established pay scale and farm contracts. Despite her innate affinity and feeling for the farmer, she could not ignore the culture, traditions, and sentiments of the land holders, which were cherished and defended as values in her family home. She was new to the problems of the country.

People do not leave home, neighborhood, milieu, land and friends without experiencing a sense of nostalgia, nor is it easy for people to transfer, relocate, and begin anew in another nation.[57] Language, value systems, customs are diverse and initially quite challenging. Celestine seemed to be quite apt in finding herself at home in Italy in due time. She was easily accepted. She was out-going, youthful, vibrant and she soon found herself at home. She had an avid and uncommon interest in sports and she played to win. Her father enjoyed her exuberance and abilities on the playing field. She rebuilt relationships with her father, his family, and her now Italian speaking siblings. She loved to sing, dance, be with others in joyful moments and pastimes. She did not impose her earlier acquired ways, nor allow her previous experience in Butte to adversely influence her new family experience in San Lazzaro.

She was a natural learner and able teacher. She was sociable, welcoming, joyful. She soon became acquainted with the families and workers living on Bottego property. She shared their life, joyful events, happy times and sad moments and was present for them in times of sickness, marriages, funerals, births. Her serene presence conveyed a warm sense of serenity. Her conversation was person directed, and her words reflected sincere concern for the situations she encountered. The local people were acquaintances, then friends as warm relationships developed. She was not considered to be "the land owner's daughter" as much as she was accepted as a concerned friend and extended family member. Her Italian may have been struggled and seasoned with foreign nuances of pronunciation, but her smile was easily understandable to all.

She was spontaneous. Perhaps her stance and presence were marked by her Rocky mountain years. The shrill sound of the mine alarm there caused hearts to skip a beat. Accidents were many, and lung related disease common. The death of a miner family member might demand that the survivors pull up stakes, return homeward, or seek haven elsewhere. Montana made heavy demands on its miner inhabitants, and San Lazzaro dealt its farmers good seasons and bad. Celestine was present when local happenings, neighborhood tragedies, and family necessities were discussed. Celestine grasped the key issues of social justice quite easily.

Teachers impart knowledge and read and study events to enhance their own professional preparedness. Celestine was a born teacher. She early learned to go beyond issues to study faces, eyes, life stories of the people she encountered.

Upon her arrival in Italy, Celestine Bottego was provided with a private tutor who taught her Italian and French. She then continued her schooling in Parma. She attended classes at Istituto San Carlo.[58] She later attended Istituto delle Suore Orsoline (school directed by Ursuline Sisters). Her daily bicycle jaunts to and from school allowed her become acquainted with the cultural and artistic treasures preserved in older parts of the city. Parma was a far cry from the city of Butte and its bland sameness. Celestine was intelligent, enthusiastic and eager to learn. She cycled along narrow country roads and new paths. She admired palatial buildings, explored the treasures of richly endowed churches. She wanted to learn something new each day when she began to visit the churches of San Rocco, San Pietro, San Vitale, and San Sepolcro to say a prayer and garner an appreciation of the religious art contained therein.[59] Her father was concerned that she might become a bit too religious. Her interest in churches was not motivated by christian piety. Celestine was young, rather inquisitive, desirous to discover and learn more about Italian art. She had been introduced to some European art in America. The Clark Mansion was not very far from her home in Butte. This home had been built in between 1884 and 1888. It was one of the most elaborate buildings in the west before nineteen hundred. She may well have visited or known about this "talk of the town" residence and its fabulous art collection.[60]

She later attended further classes and finished her preparation as a teacher at the Albertina Sanvitale school[61] in 1916. This was a time for her to make friends and deepen her relationship with God. She spoke well of prof. Bertolotti,[62] one of her teachers of philosophy, who impressed her greatly. In June 1922 she finished her formal studies and briefly considered studying medicine, but she felt she needed to take a break after the stressful period of her higher studies.[63]

In her choice of schools and studies Celestine Bottego followed in the footsteps of her sister Maria, on whom she depended much. They were of one mind and cherished similar aspirations. They had written to each other occasionally during the years of their separation notwithstanding their lack of a common language. Once reunited in Italy they were inseparable, they were kindred spirits, sisters and best friends. Celestine and Maria shared their deepest thoughts, dreams and hopes. Their friendship was total, profound, deep and lasting.[64] Together they attended English courses at the University of Pisa, and there they obtained their diplomas as qualified English teachers on November 23, 1917. In 1923 Celestine was appointed to an initial teaching position in Forlì. A year later she returned to her home area near Parma and taught at the ginnasio (middle school) "Romagnosi" until 1933 when she transferred to l'Istituto Tecnico (Technical School) "Macedonio Melloni." She later taught at the middle School "Fra' Salimbene."

3. The loss of two family members

On June 12, 1924 Maria, the sister and confidante of Celestine, left home to enter the novitiate of the Franciscan Missionaries of Mary, at Grottaferrata, on the outskirts of Rome. For her religious name, she chose "Mother Maria Giovanna" which were the names of her parents, Mary and John. Three years later she left for India where she worked for forty two-uninterrupted years.

Mary H. Bottego knew Celestine well and she understood what her daughter was going through after Maria entered the convent. Celestine's 1910 unheeded vocation call would once be placed 'on hold' since she was needed at home to care for both her parents. Her vocation response would have to wait.[65] Maria's leaving left a gap in the family and she would be missed,[66] Celestine and her sister, Mother Maria Giovanna, corresponded regularly with each other over the years.

During her early teaching years Celestine became more familiar, acquainted and involved with the people, neighbors, land owners, farm workers, and dependents of the Bottego lands in San Lazzaro. She was well remembered:

"She was always smiling, and she was serene. We never saw her upset, angry or stern. The Signorina Bottego cared for all equally with like respect, goodness and generosity."[67]

"My father was sick, and she visited often. We were children and needed attention. On Sunday she would send us food and meat for our meals. Her father, Battista, was also very generous."[68]

In the early decades of the twentieth century many people in parts of Italy had distanced themselves from the church and sacraments. Many young adults and children had not been baptized. Celestine, with tact and patience, outdid herself to reach out to all. These people became an apostolate for her. She visited people at home, attended to their needs, provided help in difficult times, and instructed them in the faith.

Celestine gave catechetical instruction in the parish of San Lazzaro. It was at this time that she informed a close friend: *"I do not feel the absence of physical motherhood, I feel quite clearly that is not for me. Maybe I am called to a spiritual motherhood like the Blessed Mother. If my interior life were more intense, I would not be so remorseful for living too much for myself. A person, who loves and creates always has something to give. I am very active by nature. At times I feel myself tied down to the humdrum affairs of the life of this small family, my spirit seems hemmed in, and I feel weighed down."*[69]

Mary H. Bottego became ill in the latter part of 1928.

Celestine took a leave from teaching to care for her mother. After their 1910 arrival in Italy Celestine gradually became the teacher, counselor and guide for her mother who was still trying to adapt and settle in the new land and home. In January 1929, Mary H. Bottego contracted pneumonia and succumbed from cardiac complications on Sunday, February 10th. She was seventy four years and four months old.

Celestine had been strongly influenced by her mother. Mary H. Bottego had traveled much during her life. She was nineteen when she left Ohio, she had spent nineteen years in California, lived in Butte for nineteen years also, had been nineteen years in San Lazzaro. Her own mother, father, stepmother and both of her brothers, Thomas and James [70] had preceded her in death.

Mary H. Bottego's life had been sorrow marked and she reflected much. The separation years were hard, for her, but for Celestine they were a special time of human, social, intellectual, spiritual maturity. Montana had not been an easy place for Mary H. Bottego and she missed her two children in Italy. She had often been ill there because of polluted and unhealthy air of the "copper camp." Celestine witnessed her mother's anguish and maternal concerns during the separation years. Perhaps this may have early taught Celestine how to love her missionary daughters from afar.

Mary H. Bottego was a strong-willed woman. Life had made her so. She was the "teacher" of her daughter, who would become the "professoressa." She was family oriented and dedicated. Italy presented her with a new language, cultural differences, new challenges which demanded much and a long period of adaptation. Mary loved her three children and she did her best that they might all grow strong, learn well, believe and trust. Celestine was the product of her mother's teaching, example, hope and steadfast faith.

Celestine had been constantly by her mother's side during her final illness. The sense of loss which Celestine experienced was deep. She now had to move forward with her usual calm and get on with her own life. Celestine expressed her feelings about her mother in a letter to a friend: *"My mother caught pneumonia on January 20th. She seemed to be getting better when her heart gave out. Few people approach death with such awareness and serenity. My mother tried to console me and she had a final message for all of us before she died. The house is now more empty. Vittorio and papà are well. They are busy with their construction which will never ever be completed. Papà is beginning to show his age. It is difficult to watch this strong and tireless man slow down. Maria writes about her mission in India, and she enjoys her work among the Hindus. This year I did not teach. I cared for my mother. It was a great blessing for me to have passed these last months close to her."*[71] In 1929 Celestine was thirty-four years old. After her mother's death she returned to her teaching profession and she continued to teach until 1949.

4. Celestine, a talented teacher

She was then known as "Professoressa Bottego." She was a fine teacher, an expert guide in English, but her greatest gift was her example. She was tall, stately, but non threatening. Her smile was contagious, her wit quick, pleasant, spontaneous and her characteristic defining trait was her serenity. Her presence left its mark. She imparted knowledge. Her pupils were enriched by the inner richness of her personality, spiritual acumen and giftedness. The beautiful transparent smile which characterized her happiness at being chosen as "Montana's best student of the year" became her trademark and "i.d.card" [72] throughout all her years. She was intelligent, a joy to be with. Her travels enriched her innate spontaneity and openness. Her students remembered her with appreciation and admiration, especially for her kindness and concern. She was gentle and caring, her teaching manner enhanced the noble traits she possessed. English was her preferred subject for almost thirty years. Generations of her students remembered her with nostalgia for many long years: *"She was gentle and serene. Although she was understandably demanding, she never scolded her students. She was our best teacher, like a mother in the fullest and finest sense of the word. We looked forward to her English classes. She was clear. She was precise. It was a joy to be in her presence."*[73]

"She was serene, optimistic, exceptional."[74] *"No one remained unchanged in her classroom. She was peaceful, never severe. Her lessons were often sprinkled with humorous quips and sayings. She was a woman. She possessed a sound moral fiber. She was able to present goodness as something to be loved. She never expressly spoke of religion to us. She never forced anyone in any way. She communicated the best of herself."*[75]

Her diligence and patience can be easily explained. She personally knew how difficult it was to learn another language from her own personal experience and from the difficulties she knew her mother had experienced in Italy. When she arrived in Parma she was almost fifteen years old and language studies were relatively easy for her even though her teachers did not always measure up to her expectations. In 1910, her mother was fifty-six, and she found the Italian language more challenging. Celestine studied her mother's reserve and strenuous effort and offered patient ongoing encouragement.

Celestine was a friend to all.[76] Celestine established warm, personal relationships with countless people and she gave a particular attention to youth.[77] The people of San Lazzaro, "her folk," still sing her praises. A wedding present, a gift at the birth of a first child recalled the goodness of the "sjorén`na," young lady in the local dialect of San Lazzaro. Comfort in a time of sorrow, an overdue rent payment condoned, remain etched in the memory. Visits to the elderly, private lessons to a young seminarian, job possibilities afforded, all reveal her goodness. People turned to her for answers, needs, requests. She was a teacher, but it was her spontaneity, generosity and goodness that gained her a certain natural ascendancy among her neighbors. She came with a smile, and generously sowed an abundant dose of serenity. Numerous are the memories which provide cameo shots of her full life. Her spirituality was evident in her good works, and in whatever she accomplished the mystery of God's love was revealed. She was also remembered by the local children who used the "Palazzone" as a place for them to hang out or meet.

"I am very proud to call myself 'un ragazz del palazzon' (a kid who frequented the big multipurpose building) ... Signorina Bottego knew how to keep us together, she made us into a family. We were poor but honest. Thanks to her, the kids of the 'palazzone' took pride in themselves. Our soccer team called itself 'Bottego' as a sign of appreciation. We played other local teams, such as 'San Lazzaro' and 'La Lavanderia.' Celestine was always smiling and peaceful. I was a young man, and I often asked myself how this 'sjorén'na' could be so joyful and pleasant. Her peacefulness, calm and goodness impressed us."[78]

"The local girls gathered at her house. She played the piano, and we would sing. She taught us many things. On Fridays we would say the rosary together. I was deeply impressed when I saw her in church at prayer. Her prayer was intense, her concentration profound and real."[79]

"She knew how to deal with youth and younger kids. She would gather us all around the piano in her house. Boys will be boys, however. Now and then we would run through the fields and tear up the lawn of her neighbors. The farmers would chase us and scold us. The ' sjorén`na' would then appear with her big calming smile and smooth things over. She'd look at us, tell us not to 'run through the fields and lawns' and then invite us to 'pick some cherries.' She calmed the situation, and sent us home happy and weighed down with fruit. She was an exceptional person, a cut above the best. We had space on the ground floor of

the 'Palazzone' reserved for us. We met there often, she gave us an old radio so we could enjoy our time together."[80]

She taught by word and example. Perhaps her concern for youth originated in her remembrance of the street-wise youth and gangs of Butte where she had grown up.[81]

Celestine published her English lessons as a book entitled, "A Short English Grammar" (Grammatica della Lingua Inglese) in 1933.[82] This book proved to be a valuable text for her students. In Butte her mother had been her tutor and guide. Celestine valued that help greatly. While she was a student and learner, she came to consider the teaching profession as her goal and vocation. Celestine now offered free private supplementary lessons to the needy and sowed serenity and goodness among her pupils.

At this time Celestine met professor Puccini, a teacher of philosophy. Although he was quite older in age, she accompanied professor Puccini, with her usual kindness and respect, over a long, struggled spiritual path. This spiritual pilgrimage and her accompaniment brought him interior peace and renewed faith.

"Whenever we observed her joyful smile and great welcome, we felt gifted." These words were repeated over and over again by those who knew her, or had her as a teacher. Her innate human qualities, her fine education, her acute intelligence, did not set her apart from others. These were means shared that she might put herself at the service of all. If at times simple folks or even "her" students felt uneasy in her presence, this was not due to a sense of superiority on her part, rather they recognized that they were in the presence of an extraordinary person.

Celestine had a constant desire to learn and share. She went to France in the summer of 1928, to perfect her French and to attend a one month long course in French literature. The previous summer she had attended a series of conferences on religious and philosophical questions. In 1931 she visited Sicily, its cities and archeological sites. She loved her profession, and she was professionally informed and updated. In the summer of 1934 she went to Innsbruck to study German and a year later she went to Strasbourg for study and to perfect her German. With a group of her fellow students she traveled up the Rhine by boat as far as Cologne. On their homeward return trip they visited Holland, Belgium and Paris. After her trip she wrote: *"I have many fine and cherished memories. I hope they provide me with energy and courage for the new school year."* [83] She attended study-courses for teachers often and planned her summers to include both travel and study. Celestine also attended courses in English Literature at the British Institute of Florence, for which she was granted a diploma issued by Cambridge University in 1938.

Things great, as well as insignificant happenings, brought Celestine happiness. Her outlook was positive and was enthusiastic. She imparted knowledge, and she became a role model for many. She contemplated the beauty of a flower, and the majesty of a brilliant sunset. She could enjoy an operatic aria, and a fine literary work. Her mother had instilled her with a keen appreciation for poetry since her early years in Butte, Montana.

She was directly involved in the parish. The local pastor often found time to participate in youth gatherings which she organized within the parish.

5. Celestine, her apostolic activity

In 1930 Mother Maria Giovanna, Celestine's sister in India, encouraged her activities and suggested that part of the family inheritance could be used to establish a trade school in San Lazzaro, similar to the Salesian Oratory in Parma. Don Calabria, a Salesian priest, was asked to direct this project but unfortunately the school never quite got beyond the planning stage.

In 1938 Celestine once again tried by making the "Palazzone" in San Lazzaro available for an oratory-like youth center. Monsignor Colli, Bishop of Parma encouraged and supported this initiative. He even asked the Giuseppini Fathers to staff, direct and operate the proposed center. Times had changed, however, local support was wanting and the center did not succeed.

Celestine had inherited a bit of stick-with-it-ness from her mother. In 1940 she discussed her ideas for an oratory with Fr. Turci, a veteran Xaverian missionary from China. This new projected trade school would be named: "Nazareth Center – G. B. Bottego." It would be directed by Xaverian missionaries and would provide professional and qualified training to missionary brothers along with the local youths of San Lazzaro. The superiors of the Xaverian mission seminary accepted the proposal on March 5th of that year. However, initial enthusiasm soon waned, and this project also remained an unfulfilled dream.

Despite these setbacks she never lost her interest in the plight of youth. She was actively engaged in parochial activities, the teaching of catechism, youth projects, liturgy and charity. Since 1925 she had supported the kindergarten in San Lazzaro, which she had also helped found.[84] Celestine loved people.[85] Hence, it is quite understandable that she should become a fine teacher and later a "professoressa." She was widely known in San Lazzaro.

The "Palazzone" on the Bottego property and "Villa Bottego," Celestine's family home always offered a warm welcome to all, and recalled pleasant memories of grandfather Agostino's goodness to the population of San Lazzaro, her uncle Vittorio's African treks, explorations, tragic death, and her father's managerial caring presence and concern for the families of his farm workers. Celestine eventually turned "Villa Bottego" into an oasis of welcome, kindness, happiness, generosity. It later became a place where the world became smaller and true human concerns paramount.

Celestine Bottego was a community person. The hopes, anxieties, worries and concerns of neighbors became her own. Her Butte experience had taught her to reach out beyond cultural background, religious affiliation, or social status of people. She had been a founding member, director and supporter of the Catholic Action movement in her parish and in its work to provide better religious education for the local people. In 1933 for the first time she organized an outdoor processional "Way of the Cross" along the roads and neighborhoods of the parish, which concluded with a torchlight procession.

In 1932 Celestine enrolled in a nursing course offered by the Red Cross. She felt that: "a nurse's training" might provide her with a professional preparation to better help the poor. In 1935,[86] she wrote: *"I am following a course at the Red Cross. I am learning much. My sister Maria tells me that a diploma may qualify me to work in a hospital in India, perhaps, I may be able to work with her."*

In 1938 Celestine accepted to teach English at the Xaverian Mission Institute in Parma. It was quite uncommon for women to teach in seminaries at that time. She accepted the task willingly. She was quite natural and her style was easy. Her lessons were uplifting and always encouraging.

"When she first came to teach at the Institute and was introduced as our new English teacher, we were impressed by her kindness and professional approach. She was distinguished, elegant, and reserved. We admired her simplicity. One day I was more restless than usual. She turned to me and politely asked me not to disturb my companions. Years later, on the eve of my ordination to the priesthood, she asked me to forgive her for that mild reprimand ... Her humility and simplicity left me speechless."[87]

Celestine was creative, ever open to new inspirations. Soon after she began teaching at the Xaverian seminary in Parma, she suggested: *"Why not collect and find a use for things discarded by others to help missions?"* She enlisted volunteers to help mission students gather used things, rags, rusted metal and the like. Once these things were separated out, they could then be sold, and the money raised could help the missions. With her own money she bought a bicycle to help pick up these discarded things and enlisted the help of some friends in Pontremoli to help her dispose and sell them. This initiative continued for years, and it provided substantial financial help to offset the difficult economic situations which the young mission Institute often had to face at home and in China.

Celestine gave the best of herself every day for years with simplicity and fidelity. It did not matter whether she was an avid teacher, diligent student, or a person engaged at school, home, parish or for worthy cause of benevolent organization, she ever gave her all. The long termed relationships and friendship she developed with many acquaintances persisted for years.

6. An angel with big wings

Celestine often visited the Gaudino family home. Whenever she arrived one of the Gaudino sisters would loudly proclaim: *"Open the doors, here comes Celestine, the angel with the big wings."* That is what she was in their eyes ... an angel reaching out to touch others. She chose to live alone, totally for God and she tried to make God known to the people she encountered. Celestine was well versed and she could engage people in matters of common interest, music, literature, liturgy, education, the spiritual life, needs of the apostolate. She considered life as a gift to share through kindness and generosity. Faith was the secret ingredient which enhanced her charm and quality of her friendship.

People who came to know her were deeply impressed by her presence. She made others "feel good for a while" and her presence offered them a subtle invitation to draw closer to God, the true source of life. Friendship was treasured by Celestine. Among the few things which she brought from Butte to Italy were photographs of her friends which she retained throughout her life. Friends were special and she found occasions to celebrate them in meaningful ways: *"She never forgot a birthday or anniversary and she was present at special occasions of her friends by a note, a gift or an appropriate remembrance."*[88]

Her actions spoke louder than words. Her days were not ordinary, they were lived to the fullest in the now moments of her life. Her deeds wove a exquisitely fine tapestry of goodness, love, solidarity in the midst of a world threatened and over shadowed by an ominous new world conflict knocking at the door. Celestine Bottego lived the words of scripture: *"She reaches out her hands to the poor, and extends her arms to the needy. She opens her mouth in wisdom, and on her tongue is kindly counsel."*[89]

7. The death of John Bottego

In the final months of 1935, Celestine's father, John Bottego fell ill suddenly. He had been the mainstay of the family, he was always so strong, he seemed to be a "man of steel." He was a pleasure to be with. He enjoyed life, was informal in her mannerisms. He loved the classic authors, and could quote passages of their writings from memory. Celestine cared for her father until his death. At times the Abbot Caronti came to visit and assist her father spiritually. On November 5th, John Bottego, whose earthly journey traversed the new world and the old, died. His life had been long and extensive, marked by joys and sorrow. Mary H. Bottego, his wife of almost thirty-nine years, had died six years earlier. His daughter Maria was in distant India, Vittorio had married in 1932 and lived initially in the Villa and then in the city. Celestine remained the "sjorén'na" of San

1944. Celestine Bottego at the time of the Foundation of the Missionaries of Mary.

Irish hillside, Sligo.

A typical Irish cottage.

1895. Glendale, Ohio at the time Celestine Bottego was born.

St. Gabriel's Parish center built on foundation of original church.

St. Gabriel's Church - Glendale, Ohio today.

Mary Healy - mother of Celestine.

John B. Bottego - father of Celestine.

June 3, 1906. First Holy Comunion day of Celestine Bottego. St. Patrick's Church - Butte, MT.

St. Patrick's School in the 1890's - Butte, MT.

Gallows mine frame - Butte, MT.

St. Patrick's Church in 1896 - Butte, MT.

1910 Butte, MT. Celestine was the best grammar school student in the State of Montana 1910.

Parma, Italy, at the beginning of the 1900's.

1945. Villa Bottego. Residence of the Bottego family, San Lazzaro and presently Motherhouse of the Missionaries of Mary.

Blessed Guido Maria Conforti, Bishop of Parma, Italy, Founder of the Xaverian Missionaries.

Celestine at 17 years of age among the grapevines on the family estate.

1936. Celestine Bottego outside the Prince of Wales Museum - Bombay, India.

1954. Celestine and her brother Vittorio.

1950. Mother Celestine and the first Xaverian Sisters. From left to right: Lavinia Moreschi, Teresa Danieli, Elisabetta Bellucci.

1950. Fr. Giacomo Spagnolo, Xaverian, Founder of the Missionaries of Mary.

Lazzaro, and her loving presence keeping the Bottego legacy alive among the people her father had always cared for. With his death Celestine remained at San Lazzaro as sole heir apparent of the Bottego heritage. This role perhaps stimulated and gave direction to her current new choices: nursing, India, the missionaries of Parma, mission awareness and her own future.

Nineteen thirty five was an important and decisive year for Celestine. She was now forty and deep within her there remained a persistent call, a grace awaiting an answer since 1910. Her mother had taught her how to ponder things in her heart and to pray the words of Teresa of Avila: *"Who possesses God nothing wants – God alone suffices."*[90] The vocation seed sown in Butte, nurtured in Parma by the maxim of the Benedictines "ora et labora" was perhaps making its presence known now that she was free from family obligations. Was this not the now time for her to allow her inner voice to edge her forward to less familiar ground?

8. India, a taste of mission

For a year Celestine had been considering a trip to India to visit her sister, Mother Maria Giovanna. She sailed for India on July 30, 1936. Three young Xaverian missionaries, en route to China,[91] traveled part of the way with her. They took advantage of this opportunity to practice their English.

Celestine described her trip to India to a friend on December 15, 1936: *"God blessed my trip from start to finish. I left Genoa at the end of July on the 'Conte Verde'. The ship was full until we reached Massawa, Ethiopia. The passengers came from many nations, but the majority were Italians. Some of these people were seasoned travelers. The spirit among the passengers was fine. I shared my cabin with a Siamese woman and a Polish lady, who was going to China to be a reporter. Notwithstanding the heat of the*

Red Sea, the trip went quite well. I did not suffer sea sickness. I spent a few days in Bombay at the very fine retirement home of the Franciscan Missionaries of Mary's on Cambala hill and at a rather simple home among the hovels of the city where the missionaries sisters worked with the needy and poor. My visit to the poorer section left me with a profound and lasting impression.

When I arrived at Hyderabad, I went directly to the 'isolation hospital', where my sister Maria was working. It was August 18, 1936, the feast of St. Rocco, the patron saint of the hospital. Hyderabad is a Muslim state, its governor was a Nizam, a member of a local dynasty which had ruled there since 1713. I was able to spend a month with Maria. It was the time of year when diseases were rampant. Everyone had to be inoculated, and I was also inoculated as a precaution. St. Rocco's hospital was located out in the country, in an area similar to San Lazzaro. It was wonderful being there. There I experienced the work of the missionaries first hand. I felt so blessed to be able to live with my sister again. It was one of the happiest times of my life.

The Provincial superior permitted Maria to spend her vacation with me in Kashmir. From Hyderabad we traveled three days and nights by train and an additional twelve hours by car to reach Kashmir. The Franciscan Missionaries of Mary operated a small hospital in Kashmir. It was from this hospital that the Sisters traveled to care for local people in distant surrounding villages. I traveled the Himalayas by horse, and made my way along endless rivers in a small country boat. Whenever the Sisters go out to visit the outlying areas they carry medicines for the sick, and they also baptize babies who are ill and in danger of death. I was able to baptize forty babies myself. On my return trip I visited some of the magnificent monuments of India located in Agra and Delhi."

This letter provided a brief chronicle of Celestine's first direct missionary experience. In Bombay she had seen wealthy homes, and was impressed by poorer dwellings. She crossed the width of India,[92] and reached the peaks of the Himalayas in distant Kashmir. She traveled by train, along unpaved roads, winding rivers. Her mind was filled with memories of places, people, countryside and human need. The Taj Mahal and other impressive monuments were along her path. Her focus, however, was more on the people, the masses, the abject poverty. She witnessed the work of the missionary sisters in the isolation hospital during the most critical months of the year. She described her trip to India as the greatest joy of her life. This was no tourist trip, she assisted the dying, and baptized a number of babies who were very ill. She was a teacher, an observer, a learner in a world quite different, perhaps seeking her way.

While in India, Celestine met Dr. Hussain, an acquaintance of Mother Maria Giovanna. Celestine had occasion to speak with him at length. As a result of these talks Dr. Hussain asked to be baptized. It is quite rare for a Muslim in a predominantly Muslim area, to enter the church. Celestine influenced people by word, and by presence. Celestine introduced Dr. Hussain to the Vicar General of the diocese of Hyderabad, and after due preparation he and his whole family were baptized. Celestine and Dr. Hussain corresponded with each other for many years afterwards. The story of Dr. Hussain was not the only experience of this kind in her life. In 1932, while attending courses to obtain her Red Cross Nursing diploma, Celestine was introduced by Margherita Guariglia to Alba Fani, the daughter of a Rabbi. The three became close friends, and they often met at Celestine's home, "Villa Bottego." One day Alba, despite understandable opposition from her family, asked to be baptized. Celestine's example and religious convictions had come across loud and clear.[93]

After her return to Italy Celestine prepared a more accurate account about her trip to India.[94] This report was later published. In her article she denounced the injustices of the prevalent caste system, she wrote about the various religions, the plight of the pariah and outcasts in

India. She mentioned Dr. Ambedkar, the leading spokesman for outcasts in India at that time. She referred to a lecture he had given in Nasik a few miles northeast of Bombay, during the time she was in India. Her observations about India were precise, and accurate. She was a keen observer, and enlightened advocate. She concluded her article: *"In the vineyard next to that of the Lord of the harvest, the fields are ripe. They await the workers of the eleventh hour. Why do so few respond, so very few? Love is lacking. We should pray that we may be less unworthy instruments to make Jesus Christ known and loved."* [95]

Celestine's trip to India was a significant experience in her faith voyage. It challenged her and she felt called to committed service. When she returned to Parma she became an active promoter of missionary causes and she did much to make mission needs known to members of the parish, families of San Lazzaro, and her wider circle of friends and acquaintances. She projected films, made photos available and enthusiastically described the world she had recently visited and come to know. She was spirited by the mission urgency which she had encountered. After her trip to India, mission became a high priority, but war clouds darkened the skies over Europe. Her hopes and dreams were once more set aside by events which began to trouble the world. The persistent voice of God which she had heard years before was stifled by the sound of German troops marching throughout Europe.

Notes:

[53] The 2001 New York Times Almanac, edited by John W. Wright, Penguin Press: 2000 pg. 591.

[54] The Bottego lands originally belonged to the College of St. Joseph in Parma. The land was purchased by Francesco and Agostino Bottego, two brothers. By 1883 the land was registered as belonging to Agostino Bottego. In 1909 the land was divided and left as an inheritance as follows: 2/3 passed through inheritance to Battista Bot-

tego, 1/3 to Celestina Bottego Citerni. In 1908 the land inherited by Celestina B. Citerni was left to Battista Bottego. At the death of Battista Bottego the land was left in inheritance to his children, Maria, Celestine and Vittorio.

[55] M. Clark, "Modern Italy 1871-1995", 2nd edition, Longman 1996.

[56] Maria De Giorgi, pg. 42.

[57] Mother Bottego, in a letter to one of her missionary sisters, dated June 5, 1959, wrote: "The adaptation to another country is very difficult for everyone. I remember how much I suffered when I came to Italy at the age of fourteen. Everything made me sad, and I was with my mother and family. It is as if our whole being rebels to this uprooting. However, little by little we become acquainted and love the new land. Many do not take this into account when considering the sacrifice of missionary life."

[58] This school was located in Borgo Romagnosi, Parma.

[59] Later she became quite familiar with the art treasures in the cathedral of Parma, the abbey of San Giovanni, and La Steccata.

[60] The Clark Mansion had white oak stairways, wood floors in each of its rooms, 13 fireplaces, fresco paintings on the ceilings, stained glass windows and a dance hall on the third floor. A short distance from the Clark Mansion there was another outstanding building built by Clark's son, Charles. It was completed in 1898 at the cost of $260,000. It was a four story stone replica of a French castle, stained glass windows, 26 rooms, 7 fireplaces, and a ballroom.

[61] On Via Saffi, in the city of Parma.

[62] Mother Bottego wrote: "Prof. Bertolotti was a person with a very sound and good religious formation. However, he was caught up in philosophical idealism. His lessons held us spellbound. We made many objections in class. At the end of the school year he returned to the faith. He died during World War II. A book was published posthumously entitled "From the classroom to God." The book contained excerpts from letters which he wrote during the war to his former students. A friend of mine, Pina Romani, who was a socialist, converted to Catholicism as a result. I believe we all received a great deal of good from this able teacher." See Maria De Giorgi, pg. 34.

[63] Celestine Bottego informed a friend of the need that she had for rest after completing her studies in a letter dated January 29, 1923. She mentioned this happening in another letter written on January 25, 1959 and although she suffered this setback she later considered that moment as providential.

[64] Marietta (Maria) wrote to her mother in Italian on August 20, 1908. She was only fifteen: "It seems so long a time between letters. Certainly you will be saddened by this. You are a mother, your maternal heart can forgive us. This delay is not due to forgetfulness, but to laziness. This is an ugly vice, is it not? I think of you always, mother dear, and I pray. However, my prayers have not yet been heard. Just

think, it has been eight years since we celebrated Christmas together. Eight years is a long time. In this length of time, how is it possible that you have not been able to sell the ten houses which we have there? Oh, if you truly wished us well, you would have sought to sell whatever we possess there and come here. It is so sad to be so far from my mother. A few days ago we received the letter from Celestine, She told us that she had been promoted. Celestine is now studying music. What do you think that I should study apart from my regular studies? Tell me what you think, Mamma. There is a strike of the farm hands here in the area of Parma, Papà had to work in the fields, and we all helped him as best we could. Today he went hunting. Thank Celestine for the postcard which she sent us. Tell her that I remember her always and I send many kisses. Grandpa and grandma are well. They are sorry because they fear that they will not live long enough to meet you. They join me in begging you to come soon."

[65] "During my last year of school... I was asked if I had ever thought of a religious vocation, I replied that the thought of a vocation was always with me." See Maria De Giorgi, pg. 30.

[66] Maria was missed. Celestine wrote to a friend, Luisa Bulleri: "The separation was hard for her and for all of us. The determination which gave her the courage to choose this austere life, will give us the strength to accept it. The house seems so empty without her presence. She made a right decision, I am convinced of this each day. Her new life is more complete and full. I feel obliged to work more and to be better when I think of her. I will not teach this year, there are so many things to attend to at home, and I am now alone. See Maria De Giorgi, pg. 40.

[67] See Maria De Giorgi, pg. 41. Statement of the Signorina Zobeide.

[68] "Signor Bottego told my mother not to worry about rent, but to care for us children. He even gave my father some land to cultivate for our need, during World War I." Statement of Giuseppina Adorni. See Maria De Giorgi, pg. 41.

[69] Letter of Celestine to her friend Luisa Bulleri in 1931. See Maria De Giorgi, pg. 58.

[70] A few years after their arrival at San Lazzaro Mary H. Bottego received word of her brother James' death in Ohio from a non-Catholic friend of his. Although he died alone, but he had been assisted by a priest in his last illness.

[71] From a letter of Celestine Bottego to Luisa Bulleri. See Maria De Giorgi, pg. 42.

[72] Identification card.

[73] Statement by Piní Marubbi, a student of Celestine Bottego at Ginnasio Romagnosi. See Maria De Giorgi, pg. 35.

[74] Statement by Professor Pietro Cavazzini who knew Celestine Bottego as an English teacher, and religion teacher in his parish. See Maria De Giorgi, pg. 35.

[75] "No one remained unchanged by her teaching. She exercised self control and was always in charge in the classroom. She possessed

an irresistible charm and elegance. She was peaceful, never severe. A glance sufficed for the class to pay attention. She did not raise her voice, nor scold her students. Her attention commanded attention, it was contagious. I saw her a few years before her death, her facial expressions had changed little. Her features were the same, her gaze looked beyond. The lessons were well prepared. The guidance imparted was clear. Her lessons were often sprinkled with humorous quips and sayings. She was a woman. She possessed a sound moral fiber. She was spontaneous, her responses were often pleasantly unexpected. She had rich human qualities and profound sentiments. Serenity was her prime characteristic trait. It flowed from her ability to "communicate well." If I were to link her with a literary personage, I would liken her to Beatrice. She was able to present goodness as something to be loved. She never spoke of religion to us. She never forced anyone in any way. She communicated the best of herself. Whenever anyone spoke with her, they felt her influence for a long time. I was only thirteen. I had not see her for many long years. My remembrance of her remains deeply impressed upon me." Statement by Prof. Taverna, who was a student of Mother Bottego in 1924-1927. See Maria De Giorgi, pg. 36.

[76] "People often lacked bare necessities, they lived in abject poverty. She offered "good news" and hope. She provided food, and at times a welcome to her home... I was only a child, her prayerfulness impressed me. I observed her kneeling motionless before the tabernacle in the church. She often came to our house for parish matters. I never saw her sad, nor angry. She was humble, non assuming, ever peaceful and serene. My vocation was born and nurtured by her presence. She was so happy when I entered the seminary." Statement by don Franco Minardi, a priest from San Lazzaro. See Maria De Giorgi, pg. 44.

[77] "Celestine was one of us. She was kind even when she reprimanded us. We were children, and we worked the pumps and pipes of the church organ. She was the organist. Sometimes we would play tricks on her." Statement by three of the youths, Comelli, Spaggiari, Grossi, given some fifty years later.

[78] "La Lavanderia" or the "Laundry" team. Statement of Bruno Torelli. See Maria De Giorgi, pg. 43.

[79] Statement by Bice Comelli. See Maria De Giorgi, pg. 43.

[80] Statement by Signor Faelli. See Maria De Giorgi, pg. 44.

[84] See pgs. 137-162 "Copper Camp" Stories of the world's greatest mining town, Butte, Montana, 1943 WPA (Work Projects Administration in the State of Montana). The kids of Butte possessed the same strange characteristics. They were individualists, they were proud of their home neighborhoods. Once a kid had survived the first uneventful years and had started to school, he was on his own. There was plenty to see if the smelter smoke did not blot out the view. The smoke was bad. In the winter it hung over the area like a yellow sulphurous pall.

School teachers often found it necessary to light their coal-oil lamps in the middle of the day. School teachers of the time were a rugged race. Their harshness was born of necessity and self preservation. Most of them kept a big switch alongside their desk. It took fifty years before Butte boys addressed their women teachers as "Miss." There were good times, but their were skirmishes between gangs as well and many blackened eyes. Parental discipline was also strict. The miners worked long hours, and as soon as a kid was old enough he was expected to help his father around the house. They had to hustle wood and coal to heat their homes in winter, and they had a thousand angles to make ends meet in difficult times. They carried luggage at the rail station, when ice salvaged from refrigerator cars was sold, the sawdust used in the refrigeration process was sold to saloons, things were delivered from place to place, they had wanderlust, and hitched rides on trains passing through. Celestine lived in a rather central south part of the city. She attended public school for a few years. Everyone in town would admit "boys will be boys" but the youth were caught up in the hustle and bustle mining camp milieu.

Celestine Bottego initially seemed to enjoy teaching boys, in a letter to Luisa Bulleri dated July 28, 1926: "Teaching girls gives less satisfaction than teaching boys..." In a letter to Luisa Bulleri dated June 2, 1925 Celestine wrote relative to the kindergarten being built in San Lazzaro: "It will be a great relief when we find some religious sisters to take care of these children who grow up without proper care."

[82] The choice of readings in this English grammar tell us something about the authoress. There are examples of simple prayers, and well chosen pieces like, "Deeds of Kindness" – these are **little** things. So they are, but we must not wait for occasions to do great things. We must begin with deeds of love. "Whoever you are be noble, whatever you do, do well, whenever you speak kindly, give joy wherever you dwell." Then we have a piece: "Home, sweet home" and the "Train" and a "Child's soliloquy" (about a mother's love), topics which were part of her life. Her examples conclude with "An arrow" by Richard Stoddard "The life of man is an arrow's flight, out of darkness into light, and out of light into darkness again; perhaps to pleasure, perhaps to pain! There must be Something above or below, Somewhere unseen a mighty Bow, A Hand that tires not, a sleepless Eye that sees the arrows fly, and fly; One who knows why we live and die. See C. M. Bottego, "A Short English Grammar," Parma: Casanova editore, 1933.

[83] See Maria De Giorgi, pg. 38.

[84] Celestine Bottego wrote to inform her friend, Luisa Bulleri (June 2nd, 1955) that the cornerstone of the Kindergarten/Monument and Memorial to local youth who had died in World War I was finally laid on May 17th, 1925, after many long years and of insistence and waiting.

[85] After the death of her mother Celestine Bottego assumed the

care of the family home. She was assisted in this by Marcellina who was employed a few months after Mary H. Bottego's death. Celestine, in a letter to her friend Luisa Bulleri, mentioned some of the difficulties which she encountered in that role. She felt somewhat disillusioned by her requisite dealings with some people. (Dec. 27,1930)

[86] In a letter to Luisa Bulleri, Celestine on May 13, 1933, informed her friend that she was following a nursing course offered by the Red Cross. In a further letter in 1934, Celestine Bottego mentions that she was getting on-hands nursing training in the hospital, and in a further letter dated June 1935, Celestine remarks that she has finished her two year nursing course with the Red Cross.

[87] Testimony of Fr. Luigi Terzoni, s.x. See De Giorgi, pg. 37.

[88] The Pietro Cavazzini family lived in a part of Villa Bottego. Rosaria, her brother Franco and their sister Sr. Vittoria passed their infancy years in the Bottego home. They enjoyed a privileged time of shared intimate family life moments which were never forgotten, and which accompanied them even in the last illness of Celestine. See Maria De Giorgi, pg. 74.

[89] Proverbs 31, 20.26.

[90] "Efficacia de la Paciencia" of St Teresa of Avila in "The Collected Works of St Teresa of Avila", vol. III, trans. by Kiernan Kavanauagh, O.C.D. and Ottilio Rodriguez, O.C.D., Institute of Carmelite Studies, Washington D.C., 1985, pg. 386. Mother passed this favored prayer on to one of her Sisters on her perpetual profession together with a handwritten note: "July 2, 1970, My mother had me learn these words of St Teresa by heart. They helped me through my whole life. I wish that these words may help you be one with God and find rest in Him. With all the love of your mother."

[91] Frs. Raimondo Bergamin, Romano Danieli, Giovanni Cailotto.

[92] Celestine Bottego's trip to India was considerable for the time. She traveled from Genoa to Ethiopia, crossed the Red Sea to Bombay. Bombay was about 500 miles from Hyderabad. It was an additional 700 miles to Agra, 100 miles to Delhi, and an additional 400 more miles to Kashmir and then the return, and it was 1936.

[93] "In 1932 I introduced Celestine to a close friend of mine in the course with us. Her name was Alba Fani and she was Jewish. Alba was very close to Celestine. In 1940 Alba was taken with her family and other Jewish people to a concentration camp at Carpi. Her dedication and care was so great that she was known as the "Angel of Carpi." See Maria De Giorgi, pg. 70.

[94] She sent this reflection to a Xaverian Missionary in China. The article was published in the Xaverian publication: "Le Missioni Illustrate" No. 6 of June 1937.

[95] "Islam and Hinduism are the two predominant religions in India. Then there are the Sikhs (a monotheistic, more militaristic community). There are Buddhists on the island of Ceylon. Parsis are spread about in the north, especially in Bombay. Catholics are fewer

in number, even though there are a number of western coastal cities which are completely christian like Goa. The Goan christians are great Catholics, descendants of old families converted by St Francis Xavier. Most of the local clergy descend from these original Goan christians. Conversions are not very numerous. They are almost exclusively found among the Hindu lower castes, the so-called untouchables. The Indian mentality seems to accept castes as a social political system. They seem to reject the idea that "all men are created free and equal." What is worst, the poor pariah are considered to be inferior ... Nonetheless, other ideas and feelings are slowly appearing. These refer to human dignity and to aspirations for freedom. How is it possible for human dignity to progress? How can the ideals of freedom be advanced? There seems to no other way than for the people to embrace another religion in which the caste system has no place. Only the Catholic religion and Islam can break the tyranny of Hinduism in India

The leader of the untouchables and relative castes and classes – Doctor Ambedkar – in a recent conference at Nasik advised his coreligionists to abandon Hinduism altogether and to embrace another religion. Which? That is left up to the free will of the individual – as long as there is a guarantee of equality among classes. Will the Pariah become Catholics or Muslims? This poses a serious problem for Catholic missionaries. The answer to this question will decide which way the conversion of the country will proceed.

The part of the country where Tegulù speaking people live – about twenty million in number – is located within the ecclesiastical jurisdiction of Hyderabad, Nellore and Vizagapatam. These diocese are the fore runners of the Catholic movement in India. The area of the Tegulù is considered to be "the promised land of Christianity." The missions there are extremely poor. This problem demands a constant meditation to see what the apostles of the Lord will do to make Jesus Christ known and loved. In the life of a Christian is it not a great gift to see missionary work carried out before one's own eyes?

At Baramulla, in Kashmir, I visited the hospital directed by the Franciscan Missionaries of Mary. I was able to assist them a little in their care of the sick. I accompanied them on their suggestive apostolic journeys by boat along the rivers, and by horse in the mountains. The Lord in his goodness, permitted me to baptize some infants in danger of death." Maria De Giorgi, pg. 64.

Dr. Bhimrao Ramji Ambedkar (1893-1956), established his leadership among the untouchables, founded several journals on their behalf and did much to encourage them to improve their position. In October, 1956, despairing of the elimination of untouchability from Hinduism, he became a Buddhist, together with about 200,000 fellow untouchables, at a ceremony at Nagpur. "Encyclopedia Britannica" 1967, Vol 1, pg. 717 by Dhananjay Keer.

56

III

EVENTS AND PERSONAGES
IN CELESTINE'S LIFE

1. Blessed Guido Maria Conforti

Three churchmen had a profound influence on the life of Celestine Bottego, Blessed Guido M. Conforti, Abbot Emanuele Caronti O.S.B., and Fr. Giacomo Spagnolo, s.x.

When Celestine arrived with her mother from America in 1910, the Bishop of Parma was Guido M. Conforti. He was a native son of the diocese and a man of extraordinary human and spiritual qualities.

In his earlier years he was fascinated by the life of St. Francis Xavier and he hoped himself to be a missionary one day. His frail health proved to be an obstacle. He entered the diocesan seminary and was ordained a priest on September 22, 1888.

On December 3, 1895, Fr. Guido M. Conforti founded the St. Francis Xavier foreign mission society. He sent his first two of his missionaries to China in 1899. Three years later Canon Guido M. Conforti was appointed Archbishop of Ravenna. In 1904 he was advised to resign due to poor health. He returned to his missionary community and native diocese. In 1908, he was appointed Bishop of Parma and he distinguished himself in the Italian Episcopate for holiness of life. His unique global vision, passion for mission concerns, catechetical instruction, pastoral care of all his people in Parma, the surrounding towns and depopulated mountain hamlets, were some of his priorities. The apostolic ministry of Bishop Conforti was influenced by the historic moment in which he lived and by the social and political issues of his day which gave birth to the partisan struggles, war and dictatorship of later years.

Celestine Bottego imbibed much of Bishop Conforti's pastoral spirit. She appreciated his doctrinal insights, catechetical sensitivity, and pastoral goals. The Bishop and Celestine Bottego possessed like values and sensitivities. Bishop Conforti often remarked that his people were not bad, but that ignorance prevailed among them.

It is said that he quipped: *"People should be given bread wrapped up in a page of the catechism."*

The motto of Bishop Conforti, "Caritas Christi urget nos" (the love of Christ is the driving force of our life) was evident in both, Bishop Conforti and Celestine Bottego, paternal in him, tenderly maternal in her. This motto fostered neighborly outreach to those near and far, the needy and the poor. The outcasts, the suffering, prisoners and non-believers were all part of his flock and of her apostolate.

Celestine Bottego taught catechism in San Lazzaro. She was a member in the Catholic Action movement and had attended many organizational meetings held in the Bishop's residence. She met Bishop Conforti on many occasions. She was a dedicated, hard working, and loyal daughter of her family's native diocese.

Parma was an important diocese, and Bishop Conforti's missionaries were working in China. He was a Bishop of two flocks, Parma and China. On April 21, 1912, a native son of the diocese, Luigi Calza, was consecrated in the Cathedral of Parma as the first Vicar Apostolic of Zhengzhou, Henan province, China. Celestine was seventeen then, old enough to have been positively impressed by that event and by the twelve annual departures ceremonies, held by Bishop Conforti, for Xaverian missionaries who left for China during the time they were both residing in Parma. Many other mission celebrations took place in Parma and China became a household word for the people there.

Celestine may well have followed the three-month 1928 visit of Bishop Conforti to China with its joys, pains, shattered hopes, human frailty, and complex reality of church building in a diverse cultural milieu. When Bishop Conforti returned and entered the cathedral in Parma, it was teeming with people who had come to welcome him home. The "Te Deum" song of thanksgiving was solemnly intoned. This prayer concludes with the words "in you O Lord, I put my trust." When the choir finished singing, the voice of the Bishop alone was heard repeating that concluding final verse again. It was an act of trust in the Lord, and affirmation of his episcopal motto, "In omnibus Christus – Christ is all and in all." The words of his motto are a rallying cry of those called to mission, and the raison d'être of every true christian vocation.

Celestine Bottego would not have missed occasions of mission education like the Annual Mission Almanacs published by the mission seminary of Parma. The missionary connections of Parma with overseas missions made the world smaller, and brought the needs of a distant world church much closer. For Celestine "mission" events, similar to that of November 9,1927, the date of the departure of her sister, Mother Maria Giovanna, for India must have impressed her deeply along with subsequent departure ceremonies of Xaverian missionaries to whom she had taught English after 1938.

Archbishop Conforti had hoped to found a community of missionary women in 1926 and again in 1928. He wrote to Rome about his wish to found a sister branch of his Xaverians. These missionary women were to be "mothers to the world" in a time when a woman's touch was needed in many areas of the mission world. Bishop Conforti's untimely death in 1931 placed the dream on the back burner for thirteen years until 1944 when Celestine Bottego was asked to consider an unsolicited and unexpected request.

In the late nineteenth and early part of the twentieth century a great renewal of mission activity took place throughout the church. Numerous new overseas missionary communities were founded, e.g. the Xaverians, Maryknoll, the Columbans, Mill Hill. New missionary publications and the "Annals of the Propagation of the Faith" brought the "field afar" into living rooms of homes everywhere. The Catholic Student Mission Crusade in America was launched in 1918, and offered great support for some fifty years in the American missionary education movement.

One of the outstanding international missionary personages of that time was Fr. Manna of the Foreign Mission Institute of Milan. His writings were readily translated and made available in the English world. Fr. Manna's ideas and zeal had given birth to the Missionary Union of the Clergy, an association established to bring missions education directly to people in parishes through their parish priests. Archbishop Conforti and Father Manna were among the strongest voices in Italy for mission. Archbishop Conforti served as the first President of the Missionary Union of the Clergy. Cardinal Angelo Roncalli, later Pope John XXIII, stated that Bishop Conforti was the most outstanding bishop in Italy in the missionary movement. He called him, Bishop of Parma and "missionary to the world."

Pope Benedict XV in his encyclical "Maximum Illud" [96] issued an urgent appeal for increased overseas mission activity. Pope Pius XI repeated that invitation and proposed that mission activity and organizations be centralized in Rome. Pius XI encouraged the formation of the local clergy and presided at the episcopal ordination of various non Europeans, native sons of "mission lands." [97] Efforts were made to adapt Catholicism to local indigenous cultures, especially in art and to create and foster other mission initiatives. Bishop Conforti was greatly encouraged by these mission encyclical letters and he did all in his power to sensitize the church to mission needs.

In 1960 Mother Bottego had testified during the beatification process of Archbishop Conforti. *"He was the first Bishop that I knew in Italy. His dignified and recollected mien ever impressed me. He made a pastoral visit to the parish of San Lazzaro. He praised and encouraged the good work of all, especially the teachers of the school of catechesis and doctrine ... The very first Catholic Action meeting was held in the Bishop's house by a small group of women. Mons. Conforti presided. His paternal manner and joyful support in encouraging and initiating this rather new form of the apostolate in the diocese was striking indeed ... I met him often at the Bishop's residence when Catholic Action youth groups convened. His presence and interest were ever encouraging to all. His affability and calm enabled newcomers and all to offer their views without undue concern ... I believe Mons. Conforti knew me more than I realized. I was a friend of his niece, Maria Piva, who visited him often. I remember my last visit to his residence for some advice. He came toward me, smiling and with his arms extended wide in a gesture of paternal welcome. This was my final and most striking remembrance of our 'father'."* [98] Mother Bottego, present when the tomb of Monsignor Conforti was opened on June 9, 1961 during the process of beatification, described that experience as a moment of grace and an occasion for meditation.

2. Abbot Emanuele Caronti, o.s.b.

The Abbot Caronti had a very profound influence on the life of Celestine Bottego. The abbey of San Giovanni in Parma provided strong spiritual underpinning for the fruitful diocesan and world ministry of Bishop Conforti. The abbey of San Giovanni is located in the heart of the noble city of Parma, very close to the Cathedral. The rich farm lands in the fields around the city were once the property of the monks of the abbey who had worked those fields for centuries. The Benedictine motto "ora et labora" (work and prayer) which characterized the austere life in the monastery of San Giovanni still attracted many people who were seeking peace and solace. This Benedictine abbey was a renowned spiritual center open to all.

On May 15, 1919 a new abbot was assigned to San Giovanni's abbey. His name was Abbot Emanuele Caronti. He was knowledgeable spiritual guide, outstanding liturgist, zealous apostle, a renown pastor. Previous to his coming to Parma he had been engaged and very active in the Catholic Action movement among the FUCI (Federation of Italian Catholic University Students.). The Abbot Caronti was also in charge of the Benedictine community at the Monastery of Torrechiara, a short distance outside the city.

Celestine Bottego and her older sister Maria had frequented the monastery for spiritual guidance and counsel regarding their life choices. The Abbot Caronti was a master of the spiritual life and he sowed, and cultivated seeds of spirituality among his disciples until they came to fruition. Under the guidance of the Abbot, the Bottego sisters, Celestine and Maria, advanced in the spiritual life and were committed to share time and talents generously for others.[99] Mary H. Bottego, their mother, was proud of both daughters, and wholeheartedly supported their apostolate and encouraged their life choices.

At the monastery they learned to appreciate liturgy,[100] savor prayerful moments of silence, and engage in pastoral activities associated with their sacred place, the abbey. It was during this time that Maria Bottego decided to enter religious life on June 12, 1924.

In the period immediately following World War I the new Abbot had his task cut out for him. He read the signs of the time in the unrest, insecurity, discontent, and discouragement among different social classes. He encouraged individuals and groups to engage in Catholic action, christian witness and outreach in zealous forms of pastoral action.[101] Catholic action initiatives were directed to the needy and poor, pastoral ministry, visits to the city jails. There was much to do immediately. On July 11, 1920 he relaunched the institution of Benedictine Oblates[102] at the Monastery of Torrechiara a short distance from Parma. In 1922, Celestine and her friend Maria Boni became Benedictine oblates, and Celestine adopted the oblate name of Gertrude.[103] Celestine continued to frequent the Abbey more often for spiritual direction as her initiatives multiplied and her social involvement increased.[104]

In 1935 she joined the "Opera di Nazareth," an organization which had been founded some ten years earlier.[105] This dedicated group was engaged in social and human development, and it promoted spiritual values and motivation to the neediest, and most abandoned people of the city. In late 1936, this movement went through a revision of its purpose and apostolate. Abbot Caronti not only encouraged the "Opera di Nazareth" but he also set apart space and rooms in the monastery where its members could meet, discuss and plan their work. The six young women engaged in this apostolate were called "deaconesses." They worked in the outskirts and in the poorer section on the other side of the "torrente" (mountain stream) which divided the "haves" from the "have nots" in the city. The deaconesses visited those poorer sections of the city where the less affluent families lived and they cared for the sick in a spirit of friendship, unity and solidarity.

In the record or journal of the association, "Opera di Nazareth," Abbot Caronti wrote a brief message of encouragement and admonition to the dedicated membership: *"Whenever the interior life wanes, the fruits of exterior activity languish. The blessing of God cannot grace and vitalize a ministry devoid of prayer."* He ever insisted that the success of the "Opera di Nazareth" had to flow from its prayer life. Celestine Bottego did not forget these words.

Under the wise and guiding hand of the Abbot Caronti, Celestine Bottego acquired a deepened and well tuned liturgical sensitivity, which enabled her to be a ready and receptive enthusiast of the liturgical reform proposed by Vatican II years later. Celestine was engaged in many initiatives. She was creative, but she experienced failure as well as success. Her frontier lived experience in Butte, the guidance of her benedictine director, the mission atmosphere of the diocese of Parma fostered her unique spiritual richness and outreach. However, the true richness and core values of Celestine Bottego's christian and mission commitment cannot be fully appreciated apart from the figure, teaching, contribution, influence and guidance of Fr. Giacomo Spagnolo, a Xaverian missionary, whose contact and association with Celestine Bottego was singular indeed.

3. Fr. Giacomo Spagnolo, s.x.

Bishop Conforti had been her bishop for 21 years, Abbot Caronti had been her spiritual guide for many years, Father Spagnolo was a providential messenger in her future life choices. Their encounter provided the final chapter to her vocation story. The depth and profound nature of their relationship were part of a plan divine. We contemplate the events, aware that God's ways are not our own.

Fr. Spagnolo was born at Rotzo, a small town in the mountains outside of Vicenza, Italy, on January 31, 1912. He was the oldest of nine children. He entered the minor seminary of the Xaverian missionaries in Vicenza at a young age. He had cultivated a special devotion to our Lady from his earliest years. He entrusted decisive moments of his life to the Blessed Virgin. When he was quite young, his health was frail. His superiors at the Xaverian mission Seminary were considering to delay his ordination.

In a letter to his Superior General,[106] he wrote: *"The greatest grace for which I pray daily is to be ordained a priest as soon as possible. I know that I am not worthy. It is not I who wish to become a priest. My vocation does not come from me, it is Jesus who calls me. I await your phone call informing me to take part in the retreat before ordination. If this does not happen, it will be the first grace which Our Lady* [107] *denies me. At the beginning of the year I promised Our Lady to take the name of Mary as my middle name if I am ordained this year."* [108] Surprisingly he was admitted to ordination and to all requisite steps leading to the priesthood. His family and relatives were incredulous but overjoyed at this news.[109] Giacomo Spagnolo was ordained to the priesthood on November 11, 1934.[110] Since his prayers were answered, mindful of his promise, he thereafter signed his name Giacomo Maria Spagnolo.

Following his ordination Fr. Spagnolo was sent to the University of Propaganda Fide in Rome, to complete his theological formation.[111] In September 1940 he was appointed to be a teacher at the Xaverian missionary seminary in Parma. He had a sharp intellect and intense spiritual life. He used his many talents generously and with finesse. He was tall, rather slender in appearance. His black and unkempt beard, quite common among missionaries of the time, made him appear somewhat severe. People who approached him, however, discovered in his smiling eyes an extraordinary tenderness and uncommon degree of goodness and humility.

Fr. Spagnolo was an enthusiastic teacher. He was twenty-eight years old. He was a known spiritual guide. Advised that engineering might be a useful preparation for mission work, he enrolled in courses at the University of Parma and later shuttled back and forth by train to complete his third year in Bologna.[112] Europe was at war. The Lord had other plans. His mission work would have to wait.

4. The war years

In October 1935 the Fascist government in Italy was anxious to secure and expand its African colonial possessions in Ethiopia. Italy joined the Axis alliance in 1939. World War II began in Europe on September 1, 1939. Poland was invaded by both the Germans and Russians. The conflict soon became a fast spreading epidemic engulfing one nation after another. Italy entered the ongoing war in 1940, annexed Albania and invaded Greece. A day after the Japanese attack on Pearl Harbor on December 7, 1941 the United States declared war on Japan. Germany and Italy declared war on the United States on December 11, 1941.

During the early years of the war, Celestine Bottego flew the Red Cross flag over "Villa Bottego," her home, which provided welcome and a safe haven for many. Her nurse's diploma came in handy also. Mothers, with heavy hearts, came to seek solace and a kind word whenever family members were victims, prisoners, wounded or among those missing in war. Young war widows turned to Celestine for a compassionate and caring embrace. The elderly, abandoned, and families in need knocked at her door. Fugitives found refuge at "Villa Bottego"as well.

"Celestine considered no one an enemy. She risked her life often times to help those in need. In July 1943 my uncle Cesare [113] *offered haven to three British soldiers who had escaped from the Fontanellato concentration camp outside Parma. They were hidden in haystacks on his and neighboring farms. They stayed with my family for a few days but it was dangerous. We requested Signorina Bottego to talk to them in English. She took them to her home where they stayed for forty days despite her personal risk. They later made their way across the Po river near Cremona."* [114] She was courageous, and able to disarm adversaries by her smile and staunch determination.

The "Palazzone" building, close to "Villa Bottego", had provided space for the children to gather and play during pre-war days. Now as the war progressed Celestine set up a place on ground floor of that building where she posted the photos of the once young boys, now men, who were stationed at the front. She invited people to pray for each of "her kids." [115]

Celestine Bottego lived alone at Villa Bottego in San Lazzaro, with her faithful servant Marcellina. She was now forty-eight years old. She was an influential person, the niece of Vittorio Bottego, the renowned explorer. She was well known, and highly esteemed in Parma, and its suburbs. Her generosity, availability and goodness were proverbial.

5. God's ways are not our own

In early 1942 a woman had approached Fr. Spagnolo for advice. She felt inclined to either enter a religious community already existent or to found a new religious community of her own. Fr. Spagnolo talked the matter over with an older Xaverian, Fr. Tissot, who gave him an answer which was clear, surprising, definite: *"Why not ask this woman to found our own (Xaverian) missionary sisters?"*

While preparing for the diocesan process for the beatification of Guido M. Conforti, founder of the Xaverian missionaries, and Bishop of Parma, which had begun on March 18, 1941, Fr. Tissot found two letters among the ample correspondence of Bishop Conforti regarding the foundation of a community of missionary sisters.[116]

One letter stated : *"The Institute at present has no female branch associated with it, to provide personnel for missions. I am considering founding an institution of this kind, whenever the possibility presents itself. I believe that an institution of this kind is indispensable."*[117]

Fr. Spagnolo returned to the person who had made the query and repeated the words which he had suggested. The woman showed some initial interest but she did not accept the proposal.[118]

The question "Why not have her found our community of religious missionary women?" did not leave Fr. Spagnolo in peace. In moments of prayer, those words returned. The question was constant, it was mantra-like, repetitive, and urgent.[119] Fr. Spagnolo talked about this matter with the auxiliary Bishop of Bologna, Mons. Guizzardi and the Jesuit Fr. Mirabelli. They encouraged Fr. Spagnolo to talk the matter over with his superiors and explore possible solutions and answers.[120]

Bishop Conforti's dream had been but an archival document from 1931 to 1942. It now became a sacred quest for Fr. Spagnolo. He had never before thought of founding a community of religious women. He was an engineering student who wished to leave for the China missions as soon as possible. However, his prayer and reflections continued to focus on this new possibility[121] and challenge.

Fr. Spagnolo would not now be dissuaded. The foundation "project" had a life of its own. Fr. Spagnolo prayed for guidance. He mentioned his dilemma to Fr. Turci, an older Xaverian missionary friend, who re-assured him that the foundation of a community of missionary women was most opportune, imperative and necessary for the continuity of the work of the Xaverian missionaries in distant Henan. Now there were two Xaverians who prayed for and were interested in this project.

6. Celestine's "yes"

War time conditions in Italy worsened. The community of missionary women to be founded was to share the missionary spirit of Xaverian mssionaries. Its members were to be dynamic, spirited, endowed with the degree of adaptability and availability, and ready to respond to any mission needs.

On July 2nd, 1943, the feast of the Sacred Heart, Fr. Spagnolo wrote in his diary: *"A few days ago I was thinking about 'the foundation.' Suddenly I thought of Celestine Bottego. She seemed to be the right person to give birth to this foundation ... Fr. Turci was surprised that we hadn't thought of her before."*[122] He suggested that she should be approached right away about this proposal.

Fr. Turci had met the Signorina Bottego in 1929 during one of his "begging trips." Fr. Turci was the English teacher at the mission seminary, and after his first visit to Villa Bottego, he occasionally returned, with other

Xaverian students, to converse in English with Celestine Bottego. Fr. Turci was assigned to China in 1934. Celestine Bottego later replaced him as English teacher for the missionary community. Fr. Turci corresponded with Celestine Bottego regularly during his years in China.

In July 1943 Celestine Bottego was making her retreat at the convent of the Spanish Sisters.[123] When Fr. Turci arrived, she was quite surprised to see him and she asked if anything was wrong. Fr. Turci spoke of the Fr. Spagnolo's project and asked her to consider the proposal seriously in prayer, meditation, and silence. She replied: *"This is something that I have never thought about, I will pray over it and I will give you an answer after my retreat."*

A few days passed and the two impatient missionaries, Fr. Spagnolo, who did not know Celestine well, accompanied by Fr. Turci to her home to receive her response. They spoke about the foundation, and Celestine listened attentively to the reasons why they considered her as a possible choice for the project. Her answer was brief and clear: *"I am more capable to destroy God's work than to make it happen."* She showed interest and support, but she did not see herself in that role.

Fr. Spagnolo heard her reply, but he was not convinced. He placed himself in the Lord's hands and made himself available for whatever would follow. The missionaries felt that enough had been said about the project to the Signorina Bottego. The seed was planted, and the Lord would provide. On the other hand, Celestine Bottego was now forty-eight years old, and her years were fast passing. Did she considered herself "over the hill" for such a demanding initiative? Was it not now the time to conclude her work, "fold her tent and silently slip away?" She continued to ponder over the invitation which had been presented to her and the initial negative response which she had voiced.

7. Allied landing, German occupation of Italy

In July 1943 the British, American, other allied forces landed in Sicily. Mussolini was deposed and arrested by order of King Victor Emmanuel III. The legal Italian government, in the south, hoping for Italy's liberation, welcomed the invading Allied forces. By September 1943, however, Hitler intervened in the unsettled situation of Italy. A new Fascist regime was reconstituted in northern Italy and a forceful German occupation of the country followed. These events provoked strong reactions throughout Italy and occasioned the formation of resistance groups and partisan military units. Groups for Patriotic Action (GAP) were formed in the cities, and Squads of Patriotic Action (SAP) multiplied throughout the countryside. These groups committed acts of sabotage within the country. Civil unrest increased, armed resistence became more organized, and the hills and mountain passes of the Apennines became battlegrounds of warring guerilla factions.

Parma was an important link in the German line of defense. It was no surprise on September 8th, 1943 when a German officer summarily informed the Italian garrison in the province of Parma that they were surrounded by German troops and that they had twelve minutes to surrender. The Italian troops in the city initially resisted but they were forced to surrender. Large numbers of Italian soldiers were deported. In the city there was a heavy concentration of German troops and Fascist Brigades as well. The mood in the occupied city of Parma had changed radically. Allied air raids increased, food supplies were rationed. There was a strong presence of well-organized partisan groups in the remote mountain areas nearby and the picturesque mountain hamlets surrounding the city quickly became a theater of war. The city population was tried, tired and wounded. Simple mountain folk, accustomed as they were to hardship and privation, resisted. They reacted to the insecurity of each passing day with their natural steadfastness and ability to devise, explore and employ thousands of expediencies to survive. No one escaped the complexity of these difficult and trying times.

People in the area were rounded up, summary executions were carried out by the Germans. Reprisals followed, and assaults, counter-attacks, ambushes multiplied, by the various parties in the cities and countryside. When Allied invasion forces broke through German defenses at Montecassino, a new line of defense, the Gothic line, was established and strongly re-enforced further north across the Apennines. In the provinces of Emilia-Romagna, wherein Parma was located, entire villages and towns were razed, and people suffered as German occupation forces dug in.

Shortly before the German occupation of Parma, on August 13, 1943 Fr. Spagnolo was appointed the rector of the mission seminary community in Parma. Food was scarce, rationing was enforced. A number of the mission students was sent to Ravenna, and the theology students alone remained in the Parma area. As the air raids in the city increased, the Xaverian community in Parma transferred to Capriglio, a safer spot in the Apennines where the community owned "La Provvidenza," a rather primitive summer place.[124] Capriglio was a tiny hamlet at an altitude of about 3,000 feet. The town, little more than a cluster of rustic ramshackle buildings constructed around the village church, resembled a flock of chickens nestled around a mother hen. One single dirt road ran through the center of town. The buildings were along the road and some were close to the edge. "Capriglio" takes its name from the goats (capre) pastured on grass mountain clearings along Mt. Caio which rises to four thousand seven hundred and fifty feet. The mountain is often compared to the hump of a dromedary rising from a distant dune. Clear water for the town was provided by fresh mountain springs. Wild flowers abound in grassy areas along the edge of the rocky path.[125]

Fr. Spagnolo, the superior, was somewhat of a free spirit. He was youthful, forward looking, and knew how to adapt and transform the current difficult situations into a jovial and positive lived experience for the students. The young community felt challenged and stimulated by the makeshift arrangements, and they adapted to the spartan existence and life style of their temporary mountain refuge. Fr. Spagnolo's profound cultural traits and acquired spirituality made him an exceptional educator and respected, well accepted guide.

The permanent residents of Capriglio and the usual summer visitors constituted a single family, many city people returned year after year to the same vacation spots, which then became refuges for them during the war. The townsfolk and city dwellers were like an extended family. The evenings offered numerous gathering spots where people met to discuss current gossip, news, and tidbits of wisdom passed on from the elders to younger generations. The Xaverian community was very well acquainted with the people in the mountain areas around Capriglio.[126]

8. Celestine Bottego at Capriglio

"Villa Bottego" was occupied by the Germans in the spring of 1944. Celestine Bottego and her faithful companion and servant Marcellina were obliged also to leave the city and move out to the mountains. They went to Capriglio. More than six months had elapsed since la Signorina Bottego had given her negative response to Fr. Spagnolo and his project. She had not been peaceful though since then. At Easter, la Signorina Bottego received a greeting card from Fr. Spagnolo. It was a simple holy card representation of the Velasquez crucifixion with a single word inscribed on it:"tutto/all." That easter message touched her deeply.

Eight of the Xaverian students at Capriglio were deacons. They were scheduled to be ordained priests on Pentecost Sunday, May 28th, 1944 at the Xaverian seminary chapel in the city of Parma. Fr. Spagnolo preached the pre-ordination retreat for the community. The intense, spiritual retreat days at Capriglio passed in prayerful reflection, were in sharp contrast with the partisan guerilla activity which took place in the war torn mountain passes above and around the city of Parma. For the retreatants these were days full of great hope for world peace based on justice and fraternity. For Celestine Bottego attended many of the retreat conferences. During the retreat days she reconsidered her response. She now voiced her "yes" to the Lord's invitation and found herself at peace.

The diary of Fr. Spagnolo recalls: *"About 4:30 this afternoon, I left the church and I noticed the Signorina Bottego leaving by another door. She was heading toward the grotto with rosary in hand. It seemed that she wanted to talk. She sought my advice. She had not been peaceful since she declined to be a part of the projected foundation. She wondered if she may not have been too attached to a comfortable life. The holy card of the crucified Lord, with its "tutto/all" message, sent at Easter, had touched her profoundly.[127] She had not been at peace, through prayer she realized that she had to change her response to "yes" if she wished to seek the Lord alone. She informed me that she was now peaceful, and that her indecision had left her. We discussed other matters. I assured her that my only purpose was to follow the will of the Lord. Today, May 24th, 1944 the society has its foundress, and she voiced her "fiat" (let it be done) to the Lord."*

Parma had been severely bombed in late April and early May 1944.[128] On Pentecost Sunday, May 28th, 1944, eight Xaverian missionary deacons were ordained to the priesthood by Mons. Evasio Colli, the Bishop of Parma, in the Xaverian mission chapel. The ordination took place at 4:00 a.m. Celestine Bottego learned that two deacons would have no family members present at their ordination due. She stood in for these families all day, including an unexpected seven a.m. air raid which sent everyone running to the shelters.

9. Xaverian students are taken hostage

By mid 1944 the Apennines had become an important and effective operational center for partisan groups and various guerilla assaults against the occupying forces. The German forces retaliated in the city and surrounding mountains. Tiny, seemingly insignificant Capriglio was visited by German troops on July 2nd, 1944, at three o'clock in the morning. The men of the village and the members of the Xaverian community were rudely awakened, herded together and forced to march to Lagrimone, a nearby town. They were placed on trucks and were to be transferred to the concentration camp at Bibbiano, in the province of Reggio Emilia. Fortunately, the driver of the truck, unfamiliar with the roads, had to ask directions. The Bishop of Parma and the superior of the missionary students were soon notified and the release of these prisoners was obtained within a few days and the Xaverian students eventually returned to Capriglio.[129]

However, the women of Capriglio in the meantime, concerned about the plight of the prisoners, turned to the Signorina Bottego for advice. Her diary tells what happened: *"It was Sunday, July 2nd. During the night, all the men, along with the Fathers and students of the mission community were taken to Lagrimone by the Germans. They were held in a field without food and shelter. We feared for their safety ... Four young courageous women joined Marcellina and myself. We took food for the prisoners, and set out to find them. Shortly before arriving at the town we were stopped by a German patrol and ordered to follow. Along the way we saw the body of a man who had been hung recently. At the German command post the officer in charge initially seemed kind, he received me well. He spoke no Italian, I told him why we had come in German. He did not believe me. We were obliged to give up all the food we had with us, and he had us searched by his soldiers. When they found nothing. He called me to his desk, apologized for the humiliation and offered me a glass of white wine, which I refused. With heavy hearts and no news we returned to Capriglio. Marcellina and I then moved into the parish house to live there. An older woman, named Filomena made two trips to Parma to bring news to and from there about recent happenings.[130] The Germans returned on two more occasions, searched all the homes, threatened to burn the village but they listened to my appeals. The soldiers left a bit embarrassed since they had made so many threats and did nothing."*

Capriglio was usually Bethlehem-like in its simplicity in peace time. The mountains still seemed to offer a secure place until circumstances changed and cast a pall of fear over the area. The events of Capriglio remained deeply impressed in Celestine Bottego. She felt that the Lord was near at hand watching out for them all and for the project now on its way to fulfillment.

Fr. Spagnolo believed that the mountains were still a relatively safe haven for the community. Hence, the students, after the ordination, returned to Capriglio until April 25th of the following year, the end of the war in Italy. Celestine Bottego remained as long as the German forces occupied her home.

10. The "crucifix" within the Xaverian story

The crucifix has a place in the common Xaverian missionary charism.[131] In Xavier, Spain there is a large, solemn cross, the "smiling crucifix" in what had been the chapel of the family of St. Francis Xavier. It is a unique crucifix. The Xavier crucifix reflects the stark realism of the crucifixion and death, so final and the joy of the resurrection. The throes of a war, so tragic and the birth of new hope on the horizon. That smile offers a rich enhancement to Fr. Spagnolo's "tutto/all" invitation. And takes on new meaning with Celestine Bottego's unconditional "let it be done." A new congregation was in the making in the shadow of the cross. Xavier, Parma, Capriglio provided spiritual roots uniquely entwined. It was May 24, 1944!

Much took place on that Capriglio retreat day. Celestine Bottego changed her "no" to a "yes." That Easter card was no simple greeting, it proclaimed hope reborn. Mary's "yes" at Nazareth was life revealing, and Celestine Bottego's "let it be done" was similarly unconditioned and faith charged.

Celestine Bottego possessed wonderful human traits which were a constant throughout her lifetime. As time passed and her years were marked by her ever-present smile which attested to advanced years attained, and life's fidelity affirmed.

Celestine Bottego returned to San Lazzaro from the mountains. She resumed her teaching and usual parochial activity as if nothing had changed. Her friends were too numerous to count. Privileged shared moments brought light to the lives of all who knew her as a friend. In the reserved realm of their simple relationships, threads were woven together with the colorful strands of humble, non assuming, loving awareness. How beautifully do the words of the gospel ring true: *"No one has greater love than this, to lay down one's life for one's friends."* (Jn 15,13)

"The end of the war was drawing to a close. A large amount of copper had been stolen from railroad freight cars parked alongside the tracks in San Lazzaro. The Fascist brigade and German soldiers carried out a house to house search in the area. Everyone knew who had taken the copper, but no one would reveal their names. An innocent man was arrested and accused. He was to be executed by a firing squad. My mother, terribly distraught, notified Celestine, who immediately set out to meet with the German area commander. No one knows for sure what

was said, took place, was discussed or with whom she spoke. However, the accused man was immediately released."[132]

The last bloody throes and skirmishes of the war were terminated. Through faith and prayer Celestine passed into that new motherhood role of which she had oft spoken and to which she had been called. Throughout her whole life she had ever nurtured her spiritual life. "Villa Bottego" had emptied out with the passage of time, now thanks to her "yes" it would become a home of a new family and a center of new horizons. She would be "mother" "la madre" and Father Spagnolo would be called "il padre" or "the father" of this new family. The world touched by that family would receive serene service, dedicated care, a hope filled gospel message, and a smile.

Notes:

[96] "Maximum illud" of Benedict XV, November 30, 1919, was often referred to as the "Magna Carta" of mission directives until Vatican II. The Pope presented the challenge of mission in the world of his time, he mentioned strategies to be avoided, and others to be adopted. In the encyclical letter "Rerum Ecclesiae" of Pius XI February 28, 1926, mission activity within the church was placed under the guidance of the Congregation Propaganda fide in Rome and encouraged the formation of the local church and local leadership.

[97] In little more than 15 years (1923-1939), nine Asian and African Bishops were appointed, one in India, six in China, one in Japan and one in Africa. Regional seminaries were instituted, under the direct guidance of the Holy See. The College of Propaganda Fide in Rome was improved and enlarged to provide a Roman education for seminarians from "mission" lands.

[98] This testimony was given by Mother Bottego in the beatification Process of Archbishop Conforti, March 22, 1960.

[99] "Celestine was a companion and friend through my whole life, in the ordinary and great moments. I had six sons, I can't forget her joy when she embraced me each time that I told her of my maternal state. I arrived with a thousand preoccupations, I would leave her arms consoled and full of trust. She made me feel as if I were the most important person in the world, that there was no other." Statement of Margherita Guariglia. See Maria De Giorgi, pg. 70.

[100] Celestine Bottego in a letter to her friend Luisa Bulleri (July 9, 1931) wrote: "I hope that you use the Missal. It contains the substance of Catholic piety. For me it is like the daily bread which the church offers to her children as food for the spiritual life."

[101] The Abbot Caronti had previously been an assistant of FUCI (Federation of Italian Catholic University students). He was the spiritual guide for a group of university students and teachers who met periodically, they were anxious to live their christian commitment more fully. The Abbot was an exceptional spiritual mentor. In 1920 St John's Abbey, which had been previously confiscated to serve as a barracks for troops in the struggle for unification of Italy, was finally returned to the Benedictine community.

[102] From the Catholic Encyclopedia Vol 10 1966, pg 612 – Oblates of St. Benedict "The act of oblation is not a vow but it is a firm resolve and public promise made by those called to greater perfection in the Christian life, and it is accepted and confirmed in a sacred rite approved by the church. Oblates seek growth in their spiritual life through the help of the traditional monastic practice that strengthen them in worship, reference, humility, stability, and more vital membership in the mystical body of Christ. The main purpose of the act of oblation is not the introduction of numerous additional devotions and practices into the oblates' lives, but the persevering consecration of their daily life of work and prayer, and their ordinary Christian family and social duties. The reformation of life which the oblate promises according to the spirit of the Benedictine Rule and the statutes of the oblates reach out toward the perfection of faith, hope and charity through that conversion of life by which they seek to become men and women of God rather than men and women of the world. The instrumentalities of this conversion include prayer, especially participation in liturgical worship; detachment in the use of material things and generosity toward the poor; chastity according to their own state in life; and regular spiritual reading and study of sacred scripture, together with faithful attendance at the regular instructions at their monastery." author A Boultwood. A Benedictine oblate in 2000 wrote: "The convent, I wish I could go there more often. One leaves the hustle of the busy shopping centre and steps into eternity where one can be still and know He is God!"

[103] "In 1922 together with Celestine, I made my vows of consecration, as a benedictine oblate in the hands of the Abbot Caronti. We knew each other and were friends for many years. We took part in various aggiornamento courses in Rome, organized by the Catholic Action Movement. She had a knack for reaching out to others. People were attracted to her. She could draw their attention. She was perfectly well balanced in her mannerisms, she criticized not, nor did she ever speak harshly. She had a keen sense of humor, she was quick with a ready response which made it a pleasure to be in her company. I left Parma and although we did not see each other, we remained

in contact. I cherished one of the last notes which she wrote to my sister Luisa and me. It read: 'After a long time we are united once again in the apostolate with the same fervor and love which united us in our youth. I would love to embrace you and hear about your lives. At present I cannot move because of my heart condition. I must stay inside in the winter. Can you come to San Lazzaro? I embrace you and greet you with great affection'." Statement by Maria Boni and her sister Luisa. See Maria De Giorgi, pg. 70.

[104] In 1975 Mother Bottego suggested the practice of the "presence of God" to her daughters. She recalled that the Abbot Caronti had advised her for years to focus her particular examination of conscience on the "presence of God." (Dec. 3, 1975)

[105] Founded by Teresina Anguissoli and Dottoressa Antonietta Cappelli. See Maria De Giorgi, pg. 59.

[106] The letter was written to Fr. Amatore Dagnino, superior general of the Xaverian missionary society on August 20, 1934.

[107] Mother Bottego ordinarily used the Italian expression "Madonna" with rare exceptions. The term "Madonna" has been substituted with the words "Our Lady" which is a more common usage in the English speaking world.

[108] See Maria De Giorgi, pg. 77.

[109] His father wrote to him: "Last Saturday I went to Asiago and when I returned home I found your letter. Your grandfather is overjoyed with consolation. The whole town is excited. We have quite a bit to do for the preparations. Expect me on the 10th of November, I will be there to be close to you and to assist at the celebrations and to participate in your and our happiness. In the meantime we pray that the Lord grant you all the graces of which you have need. Yes! May God bless you always and everywhere." (Oct. 29, 1934)

[110] Giacomo Spagnolo was ordained a subdeacon on October 28th, and he became a deacon on November 4th, 1934.

[111] In 1939 Fr. Spagnolo was appointed vice rector of the house of Poggio San Marcello, near Ancona. The climate in that small hamlet in the Marche, proved unhealthy for him since he had suffered from tuberculosis in his youth. He frequented a course of mission studies at the Urban University in Rome. He graduated with full votes. His thesis dealt with a writing of St. Prospero d'Aquitania "De vocatione omnium gentium." (The call of the nations.)

[112] He studied engineering at the University of Parma for two years, an then continued these studies at the University of Bologna for an additional year until August 13, 1943. See Maria De Giorgi, pg. 78, 86.

[113] He lived at Diolo of Soragna. See Maria De Giorgi, pg. 67.

[114] Statement by the brothers Antonio and Don Franco Minardi. See Maria De Giorgi, pg. 68.

[115] Statement by Enzo Faelli, see Maria De Giorgi, pg. 67.

[116] Letter of Bishop Conforti to Mons. Pecorari, then under secre-

tary of the S.C. of Propaganda Fide, May 8th, 1926, in Maria De Giorgi, pg. 80. "Dear Monsignor, encouraged by your constant kindness to me, I wish to inform you a project which I have in mind. I seek your advise and practical suggestions. The Institute for Foreign Missions is doing quite well. However, I have found that it is not easy to find sisters prepared for the missions now entrusted or later to be assigned to the Xaverian. I have been considering the possibility of founding a female missionary congregation in Parma to provide for the needs of its missions. I understand that most male missionary congregations have a female counterpart which completes their work. The congregation, which I am considering, could provide personnel for other missions, should their number of members exceed the needs of the missions entrusted to the Parma Mission Society. Confidentially I ask you if the request for due authorization is to be made to the Congregation of Propaganda or to the Congregation of Religious, and if this project might receive a general approval. Please tell me frankly what you think about the feasibility of the project, and offer any suggestions or considerations you feel are helpful. Excuse this imposition and boldness. With respectful greetings."

[117] Letter of Bishop Conforti to the S. Congregation of Propaganda Fide, July 2, 1927 in Maria De Giorgi, pg. 81.

[118] See Maria De Giorgi, pg. 82.

[119] See Maria De Giorgi, pg. 79.

[120] See Maria De Giorgi, pg. 79.

[121] Words from the diary of Fr. Spagnolo, see M. De Giorgi, pg. 79.

[122] Fr. Turci had known Celestine Bottego for fourteen years. In 1929 he had been sent to San Lazzaro to ask local cultivators and land holders to donate farm produce to the Missionary Institute of Parma. Bishop Conforti had encouraged and blessed this initiative, and the pastor of San Lazzaro had given him the names of the wealthier families. The Bottego family, which was at the top of the list, was well known for its generosity. Fr. Turci set out in his old truck, drove down country roads, amid the flourishing fields of this rich agricultural area. Through the heavy foliage and leaves of stately trees lining the edge of the road, he could barely make out "Villa Bottego." He unloaded a large 50 liter flask and made his pitch for a donation. Papà Battista Bottego turned to his faithful housekeeper, Marcellina, with the words: "Get some good wine for these fine missionaries." The flask was filled to the brim and returned to him.

[123] This meeting took place at the convent of the Spanish Sisters on Via Farini, Palazzo Pallavicino, Parma. It was described in the June 1966 issue of the internal Newsletter of the Xaverian missionaries.

[124] "La Provvidenza" building had a narrow door, with squeaking hinges, which opened inward from the street. On a ground floor there was a dining area, kitchen, recreation room. The few multi-purpose planks which leaned against one or other of the unadorned walls

seemed like they were decorative adjuncts. The staircase was narrow, it led to the upper floor where there were two rows of low cots. This was the community dormitory. It was homey despite the mattresses with split seams and threadbare blankets. The early morning sun provided warmth, and the setting sun allowed the dampness and cold to return to dwell within this primitive dwelling.

[125] This town was "Capriglio" and the presence of goat herds was evidenced by the pungent odors which wafted heavenward in the morning breeze. The voices of the shepherds which echoed from the valley below called their sheep and goats to other pastures.

[126] The Capriglio experience must have had a deep significance for Mother Bottego. She lived it, she kept a record of it in her diary. She used that diary entry in one of her circular letters to her Missionaries, and recalled the Capriglio experience when she found herself in Burundi (Jan. 1961) after the community of Missionaries was evacuated from Kiliba in Congo. Capriglio occasioned her response to the "tutto/all" invitation on the holy card which she received from Fr. Spagnolo at Easter 1944. Capriglio witnessed her "yes" response, it was for her a sacred place. In a letter (May 25, 1959) Mother Bottego wrote: "Here at Capriglio I pray, meditate and the designs of God seem to me ever more mysterious."

[127] On Easter 1944 Celestine Bottego replied to the greetings which she received from Father Spagnolo: "Let me thank you for your wishes and those of the students which I exchange with the same sentiment of devotion and affection with which they have been sent. On your card you have written a sublime word on which I have meditated. With devotion C. Bottego."

[128] Parma was heavily bombed on April 23rd, 25th, and May 2nd.

[129] Letter of Fr. Bonardi from Rome, dated December 9, 1944 to Fr. J. Henry Frassineti in New Rochelle, N.Y., in Documentation Vol I, pg. 55.

[130] The diary entry reported here has been edited, and shortened. Maria De Giorgi, pg. 93. Mother Bottego, in her circular letters to the community e diary, recalled the events of Capriglio as an example of God's providence and continual assistance.

[131] Conforti's vocation – he often insisted – found its origin and dynamism in his "crucifix conversations." He eventually had "his" special crucifix brought to his residence. His "conversations" and prayers before that crucifix continued throughout his lifetime. May they not have spoken of: famine, banditry, war, destruction, a martyred son in China, the masses in need of a caring ministry, a hopeful message, care for orphans, elderly, abandoned, the lonely, those who were sight impaired. Or did these conversations hint at future events, the sad China tragedy of accusations, court trials, expulsions, a strange recompense for lives selflessly expended without counting the cost. Did these conversations foresee new missions, and future openings in new lands? Did they make mention of the efforts of the

Xaverians to be an open community, with members multinational, committed to make of the world a single family. Were there no thoughts of the feminine branch of the Xaverian? Whatever the conversations, they demanded and received unconditioned, open ended, all embracive oft repeated affirmative responses from Conforti.

[132] Statement by Don Franco Minardi. See M. De Giorgi, pg. 68.

IV

THE FOUNDATION OF THE MISSIONARIES OF MARY

1. Behold the handmaid of the Lord

The gospel of Luke proclaims: *"The angel of God was sent ... to a virgin ... Mary by name ... fear not ... you have found favor with God ... his name Jesus."* [133] Celestine had heard those words often in the quiet of her heart. She had been an oblate of St Benedict and Parma had witnessed her committed outreach. Her thoughts were with her sister, Maria in India, where *"the fields are ripe to make Jesus Christ known and loved."* It took but a simple holy card, a crucifix representation, a single written word "tutto/all." Her hesitation became determination.

The war was winding down, but her will remained unwavering. She was almost fifty when she penned the words which best define her total life: *"Ecce ancilla Domini, (Behold the handmaid of the Lord). May God help me to be generous and perseverant in my resolutions."* [134] The foundation of the Missionaries of Mary came into being.

Teresa Danieli heard about the foundation of the Missionaries of Mary, at the ordination of her brother, Fr. Sandro Danieli s.x. in 1944. She was the first to enter on July 19, 1945. Fr. Spagnolo had a parchment made for the occasion. It read: *"Wherever two or three are gathered in my name, there am I in the midst of them."* [135] This proclaimed a profound truth and enunciated a program of life.

In early September 1945, at the Institute of the Ursuline Sisters, Fr. Spagnolo gave a retreat to a group of young girls interested in the new foundation. On September 13th, Celestine and her companions moved to a villa more suitable for them, in the town of Mariano, close to Parma.

The name given to the new foundation was "the Missionary Society of Mary." [136] It was a religious congregation with simple vows. It was an exclusive missionary community. Its motto was "all for mission." During their formative years and before receiving an overseas mission assignment the members would engage in a period of apprenticeship of pastoral activity entrusted them by the local Bishop.

Fr. Spagnolo set the characteristic traits for the new foundation. They were drawn from the spiritual and missionary legacy which Bishop Conforti had bequeathed to his missionaries. His missionaries were bound by vow to dedicate themselves totally for the evangelization of non-Christians.[137] Fr. Spagnolo endowed his foundation with a singular Marian spirit for which they were known. The Blessed Mother was chosen as the Superior and life model of the Missionaries of Mary. The Xaverian Missionaries of Mary were then to be all for God and all for their brothers and sisters. Like Our Lady, they were to be filled with love, joy, commitment. They were to be compassionate, just, humble and courageous. Fr. Spagnolo added a final trait, the abandonment to the mercy and omnipotence of God.[138]

Fr. Faustino Tissot, acting Superior General of the Xaverian missionaries, encouraged the foundation. A written presentation of it spirit and purpose was sent to the Bishop of Parma, Monsignor Colli. He gave his authoritative approval to the new community on November 4th, 1945. Fr. Spagnolo offered Mass on that day for the Missionary of Mary at Villa Pirondini in Mariano. He used the same altar which Bishop Conforti had used in the very first foundation days of the Xaverian missionaries.[139]

Fr. Giacomo Spagnolo dedicated much time to the formation of the first members of the Missionaries of Mary. He was elected a general councillor of his own Xaverian community on September 5, 1946 and was often absent from Parma. Nonetheless, he made every effort to follow the growth of the young Missionaries of Mary community which he considered to have been *"born of Bishop Guido M. Conforti, founder of the Xaverian missionaries."*

Celestine Bottego was now called "Madre – Mother."

She and her first associates left Villa Pirondini in Mariano on September 30, 1946. They took up their permanent residence at "Villa Bottego" which then became the Mother house of the Missionaries of Mary.

The daily routine of this first group of missionaries, was divided into periods of prayer, work, study. Time passed rapidly and the pattern for the common life evolved in a process of becoming. Mother Celestine continued to teach in the city. Yet she was a constant and active presence in the community. Beginnings are difficult for most similar initiatives, but divine Providence *"nourishes the birds of the air and clothes the lilies of the field"* and is never wanting in providing a generous hand.

2. July 2nd, Feast of the Visitation

Mary believed the message of the angel, and went forth from Nazareth as a missionary to announce the "good news" of Christ's coming to Elizabeth, her cousin. The feast of the Visitation was celebrated on July 2nd at that time.

In 1950 Mother Bottego and her first three sisters chose to make their religious profession as Missionaries of Mary in the Chapel of Villa Bottego, San Lazzaro, Parma, on the feast of the Visitation. Fr. Giovanni Gazza, Superior General of the Xaverian missionaries, presided at the ceremony. Celestine, in a meaningful gesture, made her profession in his hands [140] and then, as "Mother" of the new foundation, she received the profession of the first Missionaries of Mary: Teresa Danieli, Elisabetta Bellucci, Lavinia Moreschi.[141] Fr. Giacomo Spagnolo was present on this first profession day. He described his impressions in his diary.[142] A year later, on September 27, 1951, the fifth General Chapter of the Xaverian missionaries officially recognized the Missionaries of Mary as their "sister" community.

The Feast of the Visitation and its July 2nd date was

chosen for a goodly number of Xaverian events. The "testament letter" of Bishop Conforti to his Xaverian sons was written on that date in 1921.[143] Six years later on that date Bishop Conforti expressed his wish to found a congregation of missionary women [144] in a letter to Rome.

In 1943 Fr. Turci approached Celestine Bottego on the feast of the Visitation to seek her cooperation in the proposal of Fr. Spagnolo. On this day a year later Celestine Bottego and women of Capriglio where subject to a search by German troops when they tried to bring food to the hostages taken by the Germans in Capriglio.

In 1950 the very first profession ceremony of the Missionaries of Mary was celebrated. Five years later, on July 2nd, Monsignor Colli, Bishop of Parma, approved the Missionaries of Mary as a "diocesan religious community" within his diocese.

July 2nd gradually became "Community Day" since most community events, professions, anniversaries are celebrated on that date.

The proverbial mustard seed of the gospel slowly grows unobserved in the bosom of the earth. Similarly the tiny Missionary of Mary community grew around Mother Bottego over the years. Notwithstanding her own fifty years, acquired mannerisms, experience and life style, Mother Celestine from the very beginning revealed herself to be free, non assuming and a tireless spiritual guide. She was quite able to detach herself from her habitual ways of seeing, feeling, knowing and she adapted well to the demands of her new life and her companions on the journey. She was that single grain of wheat destined to come to maturity and silently die that new life-giving fruit might be born. She ever radiated joy and serenity, goodness and a ready welcome always.

She once wrote: *"When I think about my daughters, I am constantly encouraged and given strength to overcome myself. Jesus is good. He allows everything to happen for our purification. I think that you may have to face diffi-*

culties similar to mine. I ask for help to overcome my trials, and hope thereby to merit graces for you should you pass like moments."

The new foundation had its share of difficulties. Mother Bottego, however, was filled with joy for the gift of the foundation and the happiness which she experienced as she witnessed its growth. *"Who would have thought that a tiny seed sown in the earth could have taken root and grown so well! I am a grateful spectator of the manifestations of love in our family,"* she confessed.

Mother Bottego, however, was no simple spectator or onlooker. She was a major protagonist in the foundation which unfolded through her loving, giving, forgiving, understanding, courageous, daring, presence. Mother Celestine closely followed the humble beginnings of the work with steadfast faith and love without measure. She encouraged in every possible way the missionary thrust which was of the very essence of the family itself.

Once news of the foundation became known, requests began to arrive from mission areas for personnel. As early as October 28, 1947 Bishop Bassi asked for the Missionaries of Mary for his diocese in Luoyang, China. Plans were made to prepare some Missionaries of Mary for China by 1951. However, God's plans were quite different for missions in that then troubled land.[145]

3. Mother Bottego in America, the first foundation abroad

The Xaverian missionaries had established a novitiate house in Petersham, Massachusetts. In 1954 this novitiate house was to provide a one year religious missionary preparation for an international contingent of American, Scottish and Italian students anxious to be a part of the Xaverian family. The Missionaries of Mary were requested and they accepted to provide supportive personnel. This opening enabled the Missionaries to begin their presence in the United States. The task undertaken in the novitiate was not a missionary work in the strictest sense of the word, but rather it was a service provided to the "brother community" in the spirit and ideal for which the new congregation had also been founded. Rosetta Serra and Lavinia Moreschi were assigned to America. Mother Celestine wished to accompany the sisters, since they were the first Missionaries of Mary to leave San Lazzaro.

The American Consul at Genoa did not allow Lavinia to leave Italy immediately for health reasons. Mother Bottego, as a result, had to revise her own plans. With Rosetta Serra Mother Bottego shared the daily tasks at the novitiate until other sisters were able to come. Mother's hope, to visit places where she had lived in America, was put aside. She felt obliged to dedicate herself to the menial tasks of the novitiate routine and need.[146] Nonetheless, Mother did meet with church leaders, and tried to obtain from other young missionary communities advice and ideas for her own young fledgling congregation, the Missionaries of Mary.

Mother Celestine and Rosetta Serra left Genoa on August 7th, 1954, aboard the "Andrea Doria." Mother Celestine and Fr. Giacomo were in agreement that a presence of the Missionaries of Mary in America was opportune. This beginning was modest in size, but it marked a giant step for the young missionary family. Fr. Spagnolo described the importance of the opening in America shortly after Mother's departure from Genoa. *"This foundation is the will of God … The tiny mustard seed you sow will become a mighty tree. Every seed sown demands sacrifice. The Lord and Our Lady will nurture it and it will produce much good. We remember and follow you every day."*

The transatlantic crossing was tranquil. Mother Celestine did not hide her joy and emotion. She was returning, after more than forty years, to the land where she was born. She would be welcomed home by the Statue of Liberty.[147] America was a land of promise and sharp contrasts. When the ship, the "Andrea Doria," edged into its mooring at the port of New York, the reflection of the city, with its tall skyscrapers and residential edifices, was silhouetted against the skyline and along the majestic Hudson river shore line. The Hudson flows three hundred miles across the Appalachian mountains and upstate New York to empty into the ocean at New York city.

Fr. Rocco Serra, Xaverian, the brother of Sr. Rosetta, was at the port in New York on August 15, 1954 to meet the "Andrea Doria," welcome the missionaries, take them to visit friends and his relatives, and then accompany them to the novitiate. They reached Petersham, Massachusetts on September 14th. Petersham was a very small and picturesque hamlet about eighty miles west of Boston, where the novitiate of the Xaverians was located.

Massachusetts is the thirteenth state in population, and forty-fifth in land size. It was a key player and historic battleground during the Revolutionary War. It traces its origins to the arrival of the Pilgrim fathers aboard the "Mayflower" in 1620 Plymouth. Further west there are rolling hills and densely forested areas. In the autumn and "Indian summer" this area becomes alive with brilliantly colored foliage. The hills and winding roads present a constant changing panorama of regal reds, flame-like yellows, crimson leaves of trees of every kind, interspersed among solemn omnipresent evergreens of many types standing tall under the arched umbrella of clear, rich, blue expansive skies.

The Xaverian mission novitiate house was set back from the road. It was quite similar to the houses of the area except for the white carrara marble statue of St Francis Xavier which graced the entrance to the main house. Off to the left behind the novitiate residence there was a smaller carriage house of a similar design. This structure previously housed the horses and wagons of an earlier owner. In this building construction there was a small sparsely furnished second-floor apartment which had been hastily prepared to be the residence of the two newly arrived missionaries, Celestine and Rosetta. This would-be "convent," was given the name "residence of St. Joseph" by Mother Celestine. It was quite simple, modest and minimally insulated, but it was quiet and restful.

Rosetta Serra recalls: *"Mother was always serene, unpretentious, faith filled, living in abandonment to the will of God and his providence. She was available to all and for all. No matter what was requested of her she never appeared disturbed, she sought and accepted advice from everyone, she would often show her typical Irish-American humor. She was simple, spontaneous, noble and respectful of all. I experienced her sense of poverty, detachment, altruism, concern for others.*

What can be said of the ordinary, nitty gritty daily routine at that time? In Petersham we attended to the kitchen of the novitiate. There were about twelve to fifteen members in the community. On the very day of our arrival the cook left. Mother and I had to handle the kitchen and wardrobe. Neither one of us knew where to start. The days were full, and by evening we were very tired. I remember Mother with tears in her eyes from tiredness. She was concerned that I did not learn English as fast as she expected. She took my place to wash dishes and sent me to study.

We needed help to do all that was expected of us. We organized a group of women who came once a week to help us do the ironing. These women admired mother greatly, and they came more to spend an hour in her presence more than to iron. Mother Bottego loved her brother missionaries very much and asked about them even on the day before she died. She prayed for them, and she told me to pray for them and offer up my tiredness for the young students preparing for the priesthood." [148]

Rosetta Serra mentioned that Mother Bottego had other pressing concerns during her period in America. "Villa Bottego," her family home at San Lazzaro was being enlarged to meet the needs of the young growing community. *"Mother was well aware of the high construc-*

tion costs. She was attentive to save whatever she could from our meager stipend at the novitiate to send a contribution to Parma for this new construction at San Lazzaro" and to provide for the best possible formation for her sisters.

"Mother had a knack for communication, and she could converse with people at many different levels. Her interests were many. She brought God into everything without offending anyone, her ways were acceptable, pleasing, convincing. She was a woman guided by her heart and with a well grounded trust in divine Providence. Mother never kept money aside for eventual needs. She sent whatever she had to San Lazzaro as soon as possible. Whenever I mildly suggested that she keep something she responded with her usual smile, which was intended to instill the faith which I did not yet have and to remind me that divine Providence assured us that nothing would be lacking. Whenever we were in need she would tell me again that help would always be there and it happened as she said." It would seem that Mother did not wish to spend money for her own legitimate satisfaction, not even when divine Providence provided ample funds. She had initially hoped to visit places dear to her, Glendale, Ohio and Butte, Montana. However, she chose not to travel, and by so doing she gave an example of poverty and detachment to her daughters.[149]

The Xaverian missionaries had another house of studies fifty miles further east of the novitiate in Holliston. Fr. Franco Sottocornola, who was a student at that time, recalls: "One day Mother Bottego came to visit Holliston from Petersham, where she was living. I was a student of philosophy. I met Celestine Bottego for the first time. I kept a diary at that time. I remember very well that on the evening of that day, I wrote in my diary, today I have seen a saint. That phrase sums up my sentiments about my first meeting. After 35 years I do not believe that I have to change my opinion. I wrote those words because of the serenity and goodness which transpired from her counte-

nance. She had a sense of self control. She was non as-
suming regarding others. The intensity of her interior life
and the spiritual joy which emanated from her presence
impressed me deeply. We had only exchanged a few words,
but her words remained impressed on us on that occasion.
After my return to Italy in later years I visited San Lazzaro
often and I met Mother Bottego rather frequently. Our con-
versations were ever cordial and profound. The more I
came to know her, the stronger did my first impressions be-
come."

On July 2nd, 1955 while Mother Bottego was still in
the United States, she was informed that the Missionaries of Mary had been recognized and accepted as a religious community in the diocese of Parma. This was an
encouraging sign for Mother Celestine. On October 10,
1955 Mother Bottego left America, earlier than expected,
on board the "Cristoforo Colombo" and she arrived in
Naples eight days later. At San Lazarro her absence had
been felt. She mentioned her brief sojourn in America in
a letter dated October 11, 1955: *"This was a period of rest*
and peacefulness. At times there, it seemed that I was again
near my mother, so much did I feel to be once more in the
world of my early years."

4. The "Andrea Doria" tragedy

Nine months later, on July 25, 1956, the "Andrea Doria" sank on the night before its scheduled arrival in New
York. Two young Missionaries of Mary, Maria Grechi and
Teresa Del Gaudio died in that tragic accident. A pall of
sadness fell over the whole community of the Missionaries of Mary. Faith alone provided solace for the sorrow,
and offered some meaning to this happening. Mother
Bottego, "la madre" and Fr. Spagnolo, "il padre" both
deeply affected by this profound loss, survived by being
united in faith and in their abandonment to the unfath-
omable designs of God. A letter of Mother Celestine writ-

ten on that occasion reveals some of her innermost feelings: *"I can't dwell for long on those happenings, it saps all of my energy. However, my attention is fixed on another reality which provides much comfort. Our sisters have arrived 'home.' The Lord has rewarded their generosity as if they had worked for years in a mission field. Each of them is a protectress in heaven. I feel they help me and support me spiritually, they help me to understand others and to love the Lord and serve Him as they themselves loved and served him."* [150]

5. Mother Celestine accompanies her daughters to Brazil

Pope Pius XII, in the fifties, was deeply concerned about the condition of people in Brazil. He urgently invited religious communities to assign personnel to the church in Brazil.[151] The Missionaries of Mary answered that call willingly.

The Xaverian missionaries had been working in Brazil since 1950. Three young missionaries, Gianna Lingiardi, Elisa Caspani, Anna Chiletti, were chosen to be the founding members of this first community in Latin America. Mother Celestine personally accompanied them during their early months of this foundation. The Missionaries left Genoa on May 20, 1957 on the ship "Biancamano" and they arrived at Santos in the state of São Paulo on June 4th.

During their transatlantic voyage Mother Celestine kept in touch by mail with San Lazzaro. Her letters contain a wealth of particulars. She mentions Cannes and Barcelona, and described Gibraltar from a distance and the Moroccan coast. Her letters reveal something of her missionary passion, exquisite humanity, and keen sense of observation.

On the 24th of May the ship was on the Atlantic. Mother wrote: *"The sky is overcast, the sea appears to be* so gray and lead colored. We received your welcome telegram. The 24th of May could not have been celebrated in a better way than here on board ship. The seed sown gives promise of a rich harvest of missionary fruits. Today I recall the early days of my encounter with 'il padre.' It was in a spirit of faith alone that I voiced my 'yes' to a persistent inner drive which I could not resist. I knew I was free, yet I was not free. I count on your prayers. It is so easy to ruin the work of God by not measuring up in charity and humility toward those who have been entrusted to me, and who are close at hand. In these days the Lord invites us insistently to ask, seek and obtain. Jesus assures us that the Father will hear and grant our prayers offered in his name. I ask nothing, I only wish that through 'il padre' (Spagnolo) who guides us, humility and charity may be yours, my dearest daughters, and mine."

During the voyage Mother Celestine was everywhere present. The "Biancamano" was bringing emigrants to South America, in search of a better future. Many of these emigrants came from poor and depressed areas in Italy and their religious instruction was often meager, inadequate and limited. Her letter continues. "In the past few days we had occasion to do a bit of good. The chaplain of this floating parish, was concerned for the spiritual well being of the passengers. He knew that many passengers had not received first communion or confirmation. He also knew that those who worked in the fazendas of Brazil or Argentina would have little time to receive further religious instruction about the sacraments which are the life of the soul. Two of the Missionaries were asked to provide religious instruction twice a day in the one of the salons of the ship."

The sisters wrote: "Mother's gentleness, serenity, and unforgettable smile created a warm, welcome climate and had a very positive effect on all. In the evenings, groups of passengers gathered on the bridge to play the accordion, tell funny stories and jokes. During those evening meetings on the bridge we met many people. One of the stewards was a *fervent disciple of Padre Pio, another was a machinist from Torre del Greco near Naples. These two took good care of us during the trip. They brought us fruit, postcards and looked out for our needs."*

6. A glimpse of Africa, Senegal

When the ship docked at Dakar, Senegal, on May 27th, Mother took the young missionaries ashore. She hired a guide and a car for the day to visit this African city. She wrote, *"Dakar is a large port located at the extremity of Cape Verde, the most important city of Senegal, the capital of French Equatorial Africa. It was a city of great contrasts. The wealthy section of the city, with its modern buildings, skyscrapers, beautiful constructions, and fine gardens was reserved mostly for Europeans. We also witnessed the poor villages swarming with local people dressed in their colorful characteristic garb. We were with a tall man, dressed in his red and white striped suit, who had offered to accompany us on a visit to the city. He knew some French, we agreed on a price and we visited the city all day until the departure of the ship at ten thirty in the evening. The city was about three kilometers from the port. We visited the beautiful modern cathedral and a parish church. In both places there was a priest instructing children perhaps for first communion. We also saw a local sister, and number of others who seemed to be employed in the school.*

The driver stopped whenever we wanted. We stopped at a dispensary where there was a long line of African mothers waiting to have their babies vaccinated. Generally speaking these African women are quite attractive, they have a certain noble stance about them, perhaps this is the result of their carrying burdens on their heads. The clothing of the women was quite colorful, and they wore turbans of multi-colored, varied and beautiful shapes. Even the tiniest children are well cared for. The women are adorned with jewelry, rings, bracelets, necklaces, arm bands. Some wear veils or lace shoulder wraps. They appear as though they are dressed for a formal dance. The native villages reflect a life of dire poverty which beggars description. There are thousands of wooden huts, and often the only bare furnishings they contain are small mattresses cast here and there to sleep on. We also visited the market place. Almost all of the women come to market with a half gourd on their head, which served as a catchall for purchases made. Along the return trip the driver pointed out a small hut which was a school for some thirty or forty children who were repeating the lesson by rote, if they stopped repeating they were beaten by the teacher. It seemed so cruel."

"There were 2150 passengers on board ship. Many were Jewish or Moslem, from Egypt or Israel. The numerous Catholics on board were not outstanding for church attendance. Yesterday we sang the Mass in the first class salon... The captain and officers of the ship were present along with very few passengers. The 'passing of the equator celebration' perhaps influenced the attendance. It is sad. When we were aboard ship, our lives were in the provident hands of God. How few passengers thought about this, how few prayerfully thanked God for His provident care."

Mother continued her travelog about her impressions, feelings and hopes, and she sent it to San Lazzaro. "We have traveled a few days without seeing anything other than sky and water... Every day the clock is set back an hour... The day when we passed the equator we celebrated with a festive dinner, spumante and the traditional colored streamers and confetti. Then Neptune arrived with his court to 'baptize' by immersion all those who were passing the equator for the first time. We escaped that experience by remaining on the bridge of the religious. Tomorrow we will arrive at Recife, the first Brazilian port which we will visit. Last night we ran into a storm and sea sickness returned to upset us a bit... Today we disembark on Brazilian soil at Recife, capital of the state of Pernambuco. It is called the Venice of Brazil. We will go ashore to visit the city and we will write to tell you about our experience. This

100

is our 'new' homeland and we should all thank God who has assisted us until now. I wish I could write more and give you more details, but we all feel that your imagination will enable you to embellish this sketchy report."

7. Brazil, Recife to Londrina

After leaving Recife the ship stopped at Rio de Janeiro, the last stop before Santos, the final destination. Fr. Gianni Gazza and Br. Masseroni, Xaverians, who had arrived in Brazil a few months earlier were at the port of Rio to greet them. This meeting was a welcome surprise for the travelers. The "Biancamano" finally reached Santos on the 4th of June. It took a few hours to fill out custom forms, and obtain permission to land. Santos, 37 miles (60 km) from São Paulo, is the main seaport of Brazil. This is an obligatory stopping place and entrance point for passenger ships arriving from Europe, and a departure port for cargo ships laden with coffee and other export products leaving Brazil for distant ports.

São Paulo was built on both sides of the Tieté river by Jesuit missionaries who had arrived there in 1554. It is 2,600 feet (800 meters) above sea level and it dominates the entire plateau. From below it resembles a formidable fortress extending downward along its bordering cliffs. Cosmopolitan São Paulo is the largest city in Brazil, with a population close to ten million people. The city is quite impressive, yet it is surrounded by a wide beltway of slums and "favelas" steeped in abject poverty. Solemn monuments proudly proclaim past glories while the reality of its streets reflects the stark contrasts of everyday life today. In São Paulo thousands of people exist in real subhuman conditions. Countless people, oppressed by wealthy landholders, are obliged to leave their farms and land in the interior for a promised "better life" in the cities, new beginnings and a better future. However, their plight often worsens more than it improves.

Brazil is a christian nation. Although it had the largest number of baptized people in the world at that time, the church in Brazil, for many decades had suffered from a lack of clergy and religious. As a result religious ignorance and superstition gradually infiltrated and undermined the christian substrata. Brazil was and is a melting pot of many races and cultures. Brazil is creating and fast becoming a new humanity in which the characteristic features of the native peoples, Africans, and Europeans find expression therein. The task facing the church is challenging and encouraging.

The initial group of Missionaries of Mary in Brazil soon found themselves pioneering their way in this new and complex world. They had come to do mission work and to become missionaries in the process. They were aware of their limited and poor means, but they were serene. They put their trust in divine Providence everywhere present in the world in which they lived and worked. This second foundation of the Missionaries of Mary, outside of Italy, though small in number, represented something more than a simple gesture. It was a decisive commitment, a church event, it was lived, experienced and shared by the whole community.

In São Paulo the Missionaries of Mary were met by the Bishop of Londrina, Dom Geraldo Fernandez along with the Xaverians, Fr. Medici and Br. Adda, who worked in that area. The Bishop had arranged temporary quarters for them with the Sisters of the Assumption. Mother Celestine and her community did not remain there very long, however. They moved to the school of the Missionaries of the Sacred Heart where there were more facilities for language study. Mother Celestine, being a teacher, insisted that language study was a basic and indispensable means for evangelization and mission outreach. She made every effort to guarantee her missionaries the possibility to acquire the language, so vital to their work. She even joined her daughters in the elementary school classes, which they frequented, to learn the basics of the Portuguese language herself. Mother Celestine also made important contacts and traveled much to become acquainted with the local situation and religious need.

Due to unforeseen difficulties, the Missionaries of Mary were not able to engage in pastoral activity in the area where the Xaverian missionaries were working. Mother Bottego was determined and anxious to see her sisters settled as soon as possible. She set out to find an alternative solutions. She left São Paulo for nearby Paraná state where she traveled along, dusty and rough roads to visit Londrina, Apucarana and other areas in the interior. She believed that proper accommodations for her missionaries could be made there and that much mission work awaited them. Bishop Fernandez invited the Missionaries of Mary to work alongside the missionaries of the Giuseppini of Asti. This unexpected offer caught Mother Bottego by surprise, however, she viewed events as coming from the hand of a loving God. Her faith, which ever sustained her and provided her with serenity and peace, guided her on this occasion as well.

8. The return of Mother Bottego to Italy

The long sea voyage, constant travel within the country, the unexpected obstacles encountered, her no longer young age, all took their toll on the health of Mother Celestine. In August she began to experience acute circulatory disturbances which continued for months. This illness necessitated her return to Italy for medical attention. She was unhappy to leave her three young missionaries alone in São Paulo, before she had found a definitive solution for them. A number of possibilities had been investigated but none had been decided on. This was a new concern. *"Let nothing trouble you, nothing scare you. All is fleeting, God alone is unchanging."*
Mother Bottego left São Paulo on October 20, 1957.

Her flight to Europe made a brief stop in Recife, and from there she sent a brief note to the community she had recently left. *"My dearest daughters, I send you this final greeting before leaving Brazil. I have seen the sun rise over the ocean and I greeted the cross of the south. Tomorrow night I will see the star of the north. Thank God for all he has done well. The Lord helps us and sustains us always with so many signs of his love. You will also experience this, thank him for his gifts. Tomorrow I will write from Rome. I entrust you to Jesus and Mary,"* signed – your mother.

The Missionaries of Mary finished language studies on November 12, 1957 and then they moved to Apucarana, Paraná which became the first foundation of their community in Brazil.

Fr. Spagnolo was at Rome's Ciampino airport to welcome Mother Celestine. Her thoughts were still in Brazil, and as soon as she was able she wrote there: *"My dearest daughters, I was able to get up for the first time and for a brief period yesterday. I am still very tired especially in my head. Some say that these are characteristic symptoms of the Asiatic flu. I am grateful to the Lord and those who brought me here (to Naples) shortly after my arrival, I am able to rest without any preoccupations. The weather is beautiful here, and one hardly notices the change because of the climate. But I feel the change because of the time and family life we shared together, my dear sisters. I am close to you. In fact I am surprised no one has asked me to speak Portuguese. I read your letters over and over again. We are always united, may our affection find its expression in prayer,"* signed – mother.

She remembered Apucarana and when she returned to Parma she wrote again: *"I cannot allow any letters addressed to you in Brazil to leave without adding a few lines. I was pleased to read about your daily schedule. I have committed it to memory, so that I may follow you, be united with you and be aware of all your intense work."* In early 1958 other missionaries left for Brazil, and later others joined them. New communities were established at Curitiba, Londrina and São Paulo. Mother Celestine followed these foundations with maternal interest. *"The missionaries have just left. Each departure leaves me with strong feelings of detachment. I offer my daughters to the Lord as a sacrifice for the salvation of souls."*

9. Japan, a new foundation without Mother Bottego's presence

A group of Xaverian missionaries, expelled from their mission in China, had opened a new field of activity in Japan in 1949. However, before the Missionaries of Mary were able to make an opening in Japan, two Japanese women, Cecilia Yokota and Gemma Tamura, came from Japan to enter the community in San Lazzaro in October 1957. They had been sent by Xaverian missionaries working in Japan.

Fifteen years had passed since the end of World War II in Japan. The devastating effect of the atomic bombs dropped on Hiroshima and Nagasaki were still everywhere felt and experienced. The rebuilding of Japan was ongoing, and its struggled search for moral values and material betterment continued. On August 30th, 1959 three missionaries Wanda De Rosa, Maddalena Stocco and Caterina Loi left for Japan to establish a community there. Mother Bottego wanted to accompany her daughters to Japan, but she was dissuaded, since the trip would have been long and too arduous. Mother Bottego and Fr. Spagnolo did travel aboard the ship with this first group of missionaries from Genoa to Naples at least. A community was established in Hashimoto, a small center in the province of Wakayama, not far from Osaka. Hashimoto, located at the foot of Mount Koya, was the heart and cultural center of Shingon Buddhism. The area was proud of its well established and tenacious Buddhist tradition. The small community of Missionaries of Mary later directed the local kindergarten and assisted the Catholic community and its pastor, who was an Irish Columban missionary. Mother Celestine reserved a special interest for the Japanese foundation, she followed her missionaries there with keen interest.

10. Mother Bottego with her missionaries in Congo, Central Africa

In 1884-1885 the international Congress of Berlin, reshaped and defined the spheres of influence of some European colonizing nations in Africa. The "independent state of Congo" was established and placed under the guidance of the King of Belgium. In 1908 Congo became a Belgian colony with the name "Belgian Congo." In the aftermath of World War II, the United Nations made a concerted effort to empower and enable former colonies to become independent nations. A nationalistic movement was already quite active in the cities of Congo, the ideas which circulated were often strongly colored by European influences.

During the suffered years of the post-colonial period African nations were moving fast along the road toward independence. Congo, more than others, had been impoverished by colonization. Its natural resources had been ravaged, misused and destroyed for decades. Like many other African former colonies, Congo was impatiently reaching toward a new and unknown future. Belgium granted independence to Congo on June 13, 1960 and the government was guided by Patrice Lumumba, leader of the Congolese nationalistic movement.

In December 1960 a group of Missionaries of Mary left for the ex-Belgian Congo (later known as Zaire, and today the Democratic Republic of Congo). The group was made up of Mother Bottego, Tomasina Casali, Liliana Fantini, Rosetta Mancini, and Camilla Tagliabue. They traveled by plane from Rome, stopped overnight in Cairo, and arrived in Usumbura (now Bujumbura), the capital of Burundi on December 12th. The Xaverian missionaries working in Burundi and Fr. Danilo Catarzi, superior of the Xaverians working in Congo, welcomed Mother Bottego and her missionaries. The Missionaries of Mary then proceeded across the frontier to Uvira in Kivu province, Congo. They were taken to Kiliba, a small mission station in the "plain of the elephants" along the shore of Lake Tanganyika, in the diocese of Uvira. The Missionaries of Mary were prepared to carry out a social and health care apostolate connected with the small dispensary located there.

Mother Bottego wrote to San Lazzaro: *"We are finally in our house at Kiliba.*[152] *It is not large but it has all that is needed, a chapel where the Blessed Sacrament is reserved, small individual rooms for each sister, a dining area and kitchen. The house is surrounded by tall eucalyptus trees which offer welcome shade. We seem to be on an oasis in the midst of a vast deserted, sandy expanse. High mountains can be seen at a distance. It rains for a time almost every day, and when the rain comes, it pours continuously for two or three hours. Our Christmas celebrations were unusual and different. Nothing reminded us of our customary Christmas vigil usages, we did not even have Midnight Mass. The church here is very poor, it is more like the stable of Bethlehem. The walls of the church are made of bamboo poles, there is no door, just an opening. The people kneel on the bare earth. During Mass people pray and sing well. On Christmas morning the church was filled with children, along with men and women who carried their smaller children on their backs. The parish church of St. Joseph the worker was built recently. Over seven hundred people received communion at Mass. Fr. Catarzi visited us on Christmas afternoon and was happy to see how we had arranged the house. I forgot to mention that Frs. Viotti, Didoné, and Ibba joined us for Christmas dinner. It was a Xaverian, missionary Christmas, we had to make do as best we could."*

The small community of missionaries soon organized its work and activities. With the passage of each day the contact with the local people was more serene and familial, thanks especially to Mother Bottego's keen sense of hospitality which showed favoritism to no one, white or black. Fr. Giuseppe Viotti, Xaverian, who worked at Kiliba, recalled: *"I lived close by to Mother Bottego when she came to Congo with the first missionaries. I was stationed in Kiliba. Mother Celestine came to Mass with her missionary sisters every day. I don't want to forget any details. Whenever the Fathers passed through the house of the missionary sisters, Mother insisted that we should take something. 'At least a glass of cool water,' she would insist. I often saw her sweeping and doing other household tasks. If anyone, an adult or a child, came looking for something, she gave whatever they asked. The other sisters looked on and wondered where all this would lead."*

Before state and local leaders were duly and completely prepared, a civil war erupted over the secession of Katanga province (now Shaba). Lumumba was assassinated on January 17, 1961. Things became chaotic. Tribal conflicts multiplied. The situation worsened and the situation was aggravated by Belgian mining interests. An armed intervention by Belgium in support of the secessionists triggered more civil rebellion and unrest. It was an unsettling time, where instability became the rule, and insecurity favored havoc and wanton slaughter.

The period of apparent tranquillity for the Missionaries of Mary, abruptly come to an end. Fr. Viotti left a description of the subsequent events: *"My most vivid remembrances refer to events in the aftermath of independence. The situation became so uncertain and serious that the director of the Belgian Sucraf Company, a Belgian company, which directed large sugar cane plantations, organized a convoy to transport Europeans, company technicians and others to safety outside of Congo."* It was suggested that the sisters also leave, while the Fathers would remain. Mother Bottego believed that her missionaries were there for higher motives and initially she informed the convoy organizers that the sisters would not leave that night for Burundi.

However, the sisters were not at morning Mass the next day. Fr. Viotti went to the convent, found breakfast prepared and a note. Mother Bottego informed him that although she was ready to die in Congo (since there were others to take her place), she felt it was best for the sisters to leave. The director of the local hospital, Dr. Pugliese, had insisted that the sisters leave since the boundaries with Burundi would soon be closed. The Missionaries of Mary had been in Congo a little more than a month.

In early 1962 the situation in Congo changed and another group of Missionaries of Mary were assigned to this ex-Belgian colony followed by even more sisters a year later. The mission of Kiliba was reopened. Uvira was a new diocese entrusted to Fr. Danilo Catarzi, its first Bishop, who had been consecrated on July 15, 1962.

The pastoral and health service, entrusted to the Missionaries of Mary, was demanding. The young sisters organized themselves to meet the pressing needs of the moment. However, in the closing months of 1963 there were two major centers of rebels forces in Congo: one in the west at Kwilu led by Pierre Mulele, and another in the east near Kisangani, led by Sumialot. Since both of these rebel forces employed similar guerilla tactics, they were all called Mulelists. By early 1964 there were Mulelist uprisings in eastern Kivu province where the Xaverian missionaries worked. By April, Uvira was situated right in the midst of the struggle for long months. All Europeans, missionaries included, were caught up in civil disorders and guerilla warfare. By May 16th, Bishop Catarzi and all mission personnel were placed under house arrest. The three Missionaries of Mary in Uvira were let free to care for the sick and wounded until August 26th when they became hostages also. The plight of the missionaries hostages was a serious cause for concern.

The Congo situation worsened, the civil war dragged on unchecked. A military coup took place, President Kasavubu was ousted and Gen. Mobutu took over in 1965. This marked the beginning of his long rule as dictator.

Mother Bottego was concerned and she wrote to her daughters in Brazil: *"I can't deny that the situation of my missionaries in Congo has caused me great pain and suffering. I feel powerless. However, I nurture great hope for their release. The Lord is certainly honored by their courage and trials for the faith. The church considers them worthy daughters and true missionaries."*

The situation in Congo was resolved on October 7, 1964. A group of mercenaries and Belgian parachutists freed the hostages and brought them to Bukavu, and from there they left for Europe. However, on November 28, 1964, three Xaverian missionaries and a local African priest, near the area held by Mulelists, were killed at Baraka and Fizi in an absurd outburst of hatred and violence. The diocese of Uvira, which was young and severely tried, now had its own martyrs: Fr. Giovanni Didoné, Br. Vittorio Faccin, Fr. Luigi Carrara and l'Abbé Atanasius Joubert.

11. Mother Bottego opens a mission in Burundi

On January 15, 1961 the Missionaries of Mary, who had left Kiliba, were given hospitality by the Missionary Sisters of Africa in Bujumbura. Mother Bottego and her missionaries were hopeful to return to Congo soon but the situation worsened. The frontiers remained closed definitively and their hope vanished. Mother Bottego was dauntless. She wasted no time. She traveled around the small mountainous nation of Burundi, which is called the "Alps of Africa" and shares borders with Tanzania, Congo and Lake Tanganyika. On February 25th Mother Celestine, accompanied by Rosetta Mancini, set out for

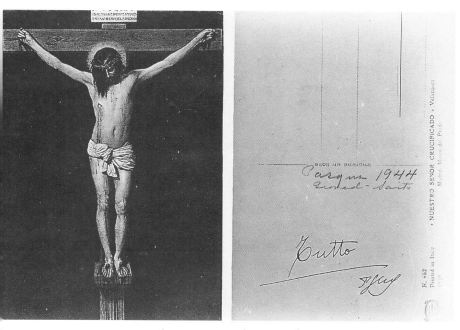

Easter 1944. Greeting sent by Fr. Spagnolo to Mother Bottego.

Capriglio - Parma. Along this road her initial "no" was transformed into a determined "yes".

August 7, 1954. Mother Bottego, Fr. Spagnolo and Rosetta Serra on the day of the departure of the Missionaries of Mary for USA.

Mother Celestine with the first directive board of the Missionaries of Mary. From left to right: Gianna Lingiardi, Liliana Rossi, Mariapia Arienti, Iole Rolli.

1956. Maria Grechi e Teresa Del Gaudio lost at sea aboard the Andrea Doria.

1957. Villa Bottego undergoes its first face lift.

1957. Mother Celestine with her daughters Gianna Lingiardi, Elisa Caspani e Anna Chiletti on their way to Brazil.

1958. Mother Celestine bids farewell to Maria Luisa Dallari and Ersilia Picci leaving for America.

1959. Card. Gregorio Pietro Agagianian, Prefect of the Congregation for the Evangelization of Peoples, visited the Motherhouse of the Missionaries of Mary.

August 30, 1959. Mother Celestine accompanied (from left to right) Caterina Loi, Wanda De Rosa, Maddalena Stocco to the ship when they left for Japan.

1960. The arrival of Mother and her first sisters to Uvira, Kivu Province - Congo.

1964. Fr. Castelli, Superior general of Xaverian Missionaries, with Mother Bottego and Fr. Spagnolo on occasion of grant of approval of Missionaries of Mary as a Pontifical Missionary Foundation within the church.

1968. Mother Bottego with her sister Mother Maria Giovanna, a Missionary in India for 42 years, and their brother Vittorio.

December 20, 1977. Last photo of Mother Bottego with Fr. Spagnolo.

Capriglio, "La Provvidenza".

Mother Bottego and Fr. Spagnolo, shortly before his death in 1978.

The Motherhouse of the Missionaries of Mary today.

Simply Mother. She tired not in writing to her daughters world wide.

1979. Mother Celestine greets sisters Mariapia Arienti and Lina Perrini, leaving for Congo.

Mother Celestine welcomes sisters home, Stephanie Loi from America and Maria Iwase from Japan.

1980. One of the last photos. Serenely awaiting her call home to the Lord.

December 20, 1979. Last birthday of Mother Celestine with her ever present smile!

August 22, 1980. Eucharistic celebration in Cathedral of Parma.

August 22, 1980. Her sisters bid her farewell in the community Chapel.

August 22, 1980. The last farewell in Cathedral of Parma.

Kibungu, a mission in Rwanda where they met a veteran Missionary of Africa [153] who was quite familiar with the area and local missions. Not finding the answers they sought, they returned to Bujumbura three days later. They set out again, this time for Rumonge and Bururi, two towns in Burundi.

Bururi was a mountain town, located between the grasslands and the forest. Mission activity in that area had been pioneered by Belgian Missionaries of Africa. Since an urgent need for additional mission personnel existed in that area, Mother Bottego decided that this was the place for her displaced missionary sisters and she committed their service to that area of Burundi. Mother Bottego returned to Italy on April 6, 1961. She had been in Africa four short, tense and busy months. It was a time of trial and a moment of new beginnings. As this turbulent period in central Africa came to an end the Sacred Congregation of Propaganda Fide, in 1964, granted the Missionaries of Mary the "decretum laudis" by which they were recognized as a religious congregation of pontifical right within the church. The world was rapidly changing, former colonies were becoming independent nations, the Vatican council was taking place.

12. Mother Bottego, a musician at heart

Mother Bottego loved music, and she allowed music to give direction to her life. When she returned from troubled Congo in 1961 with a heavy heart she found solace in a brief reflection of Pope John XXIII: *"The church continues to sing out with joy to the Lord, despite moments of persecution and strife..."* And even though the nationalities in the church are many, its hymn of praise is harmonious and one. Mother added: *"Similarly our own community hymn of praise and thanks should be harmonious and one like that of the church. May Our Lady, our model, help us grow along with the church in this spirit."* [154]

She listened to a TV transmission of a concert, given in the presence of Pope John XXIII, and she expressed the wish that the Missionaries of Mary community present itself as a single "note" in the ongoing concert of the church. The community "note" should resound perfectly so that the symphony of the entire church might be harmonious. She further observed.

The "note" of the universal church resounds in unison notwithstanding the rich diversity of peoples of various nations and cultures assembled therein. In like fashion the "note" of each religious community should resound in unison and universality. The "note" of the Missionaries of Mary should reflect the harmony of all individual community members, and respect their diverse temperament, culture, education, amidst the single shared dream adopted by all as a life project.

Mother Bottego viewed this "note" as representative of people of gifts diverse, held together in a single family by rich ties of shared and professed faith. This community "note" peals and proclaims "unity amidst diversity" in the congregation and wherever missionaries carry out their apostolate of loving care.[155] Mother Bottego, often and even on her deathbed, repeated this concept, to be a "note" and "a part" of the church's common hymn of praise to God.

In 1966 Mother Bottego, on the eve of the first Chapter of the Missionaries of Mary, returned to this theme. She recalled: *"Anyone who has studied the piano knows that it is not enough to love music and read notes in order to play the piano well. The pianist must patiently practice and acquire tried techniques to educate the muscles of the hands to present the selected piece well."* [156]

Although Mother Bottego had been "foundress" and guide for the Missionaries of Mary for about twenty years, she was remembered by many as "Signorina Bottego." Maestro Cavazzini, an able pianist and composer, knew Mother Bottego quite well from 1948 and he remarked: [157] *"It seemed that she pondered all in God's prov-*

idence and love. I believe she was always profoundly in love with God. Her sense of humanity and exquisite refinement were singular. Nothing surprised her, nothing disturbed her serene stance. For her, all things were possible for those who had faith. She loved totally and sincerely... She made herself available to serve others in a very non assuming natural ways. She expressed her loving concern in ways that made me think that I was the only one she was concerned about. One day she told me: 'Maybe in paradise we will discover why we care for each other and wish each other well.' She was always intimately attuned to the will of God. She was attentive and discreet, and she never placed herself between God and another... The example of her shared sincere affection and total self giving taught me the secret of the soul of the apostolate, which is the capacity to lose oneself in the service of others. She was ever magnanimous, and her coherence was singular, both found a maturity of expression in her. The expression of her love was natural and human, and it pointed to God. She could be compared to a symphonic poem, with an infinite variety of steps and passages, subdued, without too many evident themes." [158]

13. Mother followed the work of the Second Vatican Council closely

Pope John XXIII had been elected on October 28th, 1958. On that very day the second contingent of the Xaverian missionary priests assigned to Congo left Rome's Ciampino airport for Central Africa. The reign of John XXIII was relatively brief, yet under his leadership the church enjoyed an exceptional season of renewal and openness to the world. On January 25, 1959 the world was caught by surprise when the Holy Father announced a synod for the diocese of Rome, the reform of the Canon Law, and an ecumenical council for the universal church. The Pope proposed two major topics for the ecumenical council, aggiornamento of the church's worldwide apostolate in the modern world, and the unity of all Christians.

Mother Bottego focused on the themes taken up by the Council documents. The preparation for the council had been long, detailed, and far reaching. The Ecumenical Council was solemnly opened by Pope John XXIII on October 11, 1962. Mother Bottego attended that opening session. Pope Paul VI presided at its closing session on December 8, 1965. He proved to be tireless in dialogue, and an outstanding mediator among different factions during the Council and in its aftermath.

The Council documents reached far beyond the initial expectations. They provided a dynamic regeneration and profound changes which touched every aspect of the life of the church. The open window of John XXIII did bring a breath of fresh air to the church, and brushed its edifice free of the accumulated dust of past centuries. The great constitutions "Lumen Gentium" (on the Church) and "Gaudium et Spes" (the Church in the modern world), the decrees on Ecumenism, non-Christian religions, religious freedom, touched the church profoundly in its relationship with the world. An additional two constitutions, "Dei Verbum" (on revelation) and "Sacrosanctum Concilium" (on the liturgy), were directed to the church itself. Other decrees on religious life, priesthood, missionary activity and the vocation of the laity, brought about profound and far reaching changes as well.

The process of renewal initiated by the Council was far reaching. Institutes and religious communities were insistently invited to review their constitutions, seek new and creative modes to re-discover their charism.

Mother Celestine intensely followed and lived council events. She welcomed its teachings and made the spirit of the Council her own. Under the wise and guiding hand of the Abbate Caronti she had earlier deepened and fine tuned her liturgical sensitivity. She was pleased with new reforms taking place within the church. Her natural ecumenical outreach found encouragement in the council directives and events. She was profoundly moved by the prophetic gestures of Paul VI in his meetings with the Archbishop of Canterbury in 1966 and Patriarch Athenagoras in 1967.

Many years earlier when Celestine Bottego attended the University of Florence, one of her teachers and friends was Miss Dorothy Benton. Miss Benton married Rev. Kent White, an Anglican clergyman, and later she herself became a Catholic. The Whites visited Italy on a number of occasions. In the post council era of change and ecumenism Mother Celestine welcomed her friends, the Whites, to Villa Bottego in San Lazzaro with her characteristic magnanimity and openness. She obtained permission, from the Bishop of Parma, for the Rev. Kent White to celebrate Mass at "Villa Bottego." This gesture made a profound and lasting impression on the somewhat austere Anglican pastor. Her simple gesture said more than many ecumenical texts.[159]

Fr. Franco Sottocornola, a liturgist, wrote: *"I was a friend, a son. In that role I can say that I was privy to some of Celestine's confidences and I came to know something of her heart. Her spirituality was always nurtured by the liturgy. In her early years she was privileged to have Abbot Emanuele Caronti, a great apostle of liturgical renewal in Italy, as her master and guide. During the years of the post conciliar reform I found her to be always open and enthusiastic regarding the liturgical changes which were proposed as part of the reform, changes which we sought to implement. She constantly asked for information, news, explanations in this regard, which revealed her deep understanding of having an intense liturgical life. I can say that the liturgy, and especially the Mass, were at the center of her spiritual life. I believe that even our friendship was centered and related to our common interest in the liturgy. A characteristic of her spirituality was her openness to ecumenism. Now and then she spoke of Butte, Montana, where she grew up and recalled her early childhood experi-*

ences with protestants. From that time on she had nurtured a deep desire for the unity of all Christians, and she followed the initiatives and progress of the ecumenical movement.[160]

Mother Bottego attended lecture series on council topics and renewal which were presented at the Xaverian Theology house in Parma. She was also present at "Villa Bottego" at the lectures provided by faculty members of the Xaverian seminary for the Missionaries of Mary in formation. She was enthusiastic about the work of the Council and looked forward to its effect on the church in the world. She was personally touched by the spirit of renewal on different levels of her life. It was in this new ecclesial climate, charged with the fervor of the Council, reforms initiated, new theological projections, rich insights in Scripture study, that the young Institute of the Missionaries of Mary prepared to celebrate its first General Chapter.

14. The inauguration of the Motherhouse at San Lazzaro

Over the years the Missionaries of Mary had increased in number. The community was growing and enthusiasm was high. Young missionaries were steadily being prepared for their mission through study, prayer and work. The Chapter would evaluate the past and program the future.

Mother Bottego never lost her human touch in her contact with her neighbors, friends and supporters. Villa Bottego had become the Motherhouse of the Missionaries of Mary. Its space was re-distributed, and alterations made, as the community grew. A four storied extension was added over the years, and the earth from the new foundations provided the dirt for the hill on which a Shrine to Our Lady of Fatima was built to grace the entrance to the new familial home of the Missionaries of

Mary. Yet, the original structural lines of the "Bottego family homestead" were preserved. It continues to bear witness to the exceptional Bottego family and to the more remarkable on going story of outreach, mission, dedication, carried out by the daughters of Mother Bottego.

In the months before the general chapter the construction had been concluded. Mother spoke at the inauguration of the place she called "home." She acknowledged the generosity of the benefactors in making the enlarged Motherhouse a reality. When faced with the high estimate for the construction Mother Bottego responded to those who questioned her: *"I know what the costs will be. However, I have great trust and faith. I know that I can count upon loans without time limits from a Bank which has never known failure, divine Providence. Providence has not failed me now. The building was absolutely necessary."* Mother Bottego, on that occasion, revealed a secret when she stated: *"From the very beginning of the Missionaries of Mary we placed all of our economic problems in the hands of St. Joseph. God entrusted him with the Holy Family, the church has adopted him as its Patron, and we named him Treasurer of our Society. I can honestly tell you that we have tangibly felt his paternal and all but miraculous assistance in these years.*

This demands faith, much faith, the faith which is the substance of things hoped for. It is that faith which enabled our hopes to become reality.

Faith has conducted to this place many young women desirous to dedicate themselves to the service of God and our neighbors in mission. This faith creates and sustains works by demanding perseverance in the midst of difficulties. Glance over the story of our missions and you will see how the Missionaries are called to live their faith. May this 'Inauguration day celebration' be for you and us a singular hymn of thanksgiving to divine Providence." These remarks cast much light on her preferred beatitude: *"Blessed are you because you have believed!"* Her strong arm clasp accentuated and confirmed that oft repeated and lived phrase.[161]

Notes:

[133] Lk 1,26ff.

[134] On May 24, 1944. Apart from the initial Latin words, her decisive words were written in English.

[135] Mt 18,20.

[136] "Societas Missionalis Mariae."

[137] Bishop Conforti had written: "The primary goal of the pious society of St. Francis Xavier is the sanctification of its members by means of the profession of simple vows of poverty, chastity and obedience. Its particular goal is the preaching of the Gospel in non-christian lands, in keeping with the mandate of Christ: "Euntes in mundum universum, praedicate Evangelium omni creaturae" (Go, therefore, to the whole world and preach the gospel to every creature, Mk 16,15). The society takes inspiration from the glorious apostle of the Indies, and is ready to receive from the Vicar of Christ, through the Sacred Congregation of Propaganda Fide, whatever missions among non-christians that he wishes to assign to it."

[138] Faithful to his own spiritual experience, Fr. Spagnolo added the abandonment to the mercy and omnipotence of God as an additional trait in the spirituality of the Missionaries of Mary.

[139] The altar was used on December 3, 1895 at Borgo Leon d'Oro, Parma.

[140] Mother Bottego took as her number of profession #2. In a letter of July 5, 1957 she wrote: "Another way to foster unity can be found in the Blessed Mother: She is our true Mother and Superior. You recall that She was chosen from the very beginning of our foundation to be #1. She is the one who has enabled our community to remain alive through so many material and spiritual difficulties, and through her assistance, She will see our community grow."

[141] On that occasion Fr. Gazza remarked: "What we have witnessed here today with our own eyes, what we have heard with our own ears here, has profoundly touched our hearts. Mother and daughters have made their religious, missionary profession. Who of us doubts that the spirit of Bishop Conforti is not here present. Through his written, oral, presence, teaching, all of which is a part of his total heritage, he indicated the way to follow, the road to walk, in order to attain our heavenly goal."

[142] "Jesus, I cannot conclude this glorious day of mercy without giving thanks, recognition and praise to you for your goodness and divine condescension. I thank you, Lord, for all that has taken place

on this great day and for the ways by which I am allowed to serve your glory, to the joy of my superiors and my holy, respected sisters. I thank you Lord, for these four professed sisters, five novices, and ten postulants. They are yours, Jesus. You have entrusted them to me, but they are yours. I ask nothing but the grace to correspond with your wishes.

I think of you, my dear ones, which I dare not call daughters, because I am not worthy to be called your father. To you present today, and to those who will join in years to come, I offer a song of praise to the divine mercy of God. To all of you who are consecrated to the Mother of mercy and to the infinite, merciful love of God, remember, it is in God's name that I entrust you with a mission. You are always to be, through the centuries, an incessant song and a victim of praise and glory to divine mercy for all that has been and continues to be accomplished for our good and sanctification, and for that of all humankind forever." See Maria De Giorgi, pg 101.

[143] In that letter he briefly described his spiritual legacy: "Permit me to express my remarks in this final wish. May the distinguishing trait of the present and future members of the Society result from three of its common and essential components. First component is that spirit of living faith by which we are able to see God, seek God, love God in all and which heightens our eagerness to propagate his kingdom everywhere. The second component is that prompt, selfless, constant spirit of obedience in all without measure which attains the victories promised by the Lord. The third component is a deep love, intense love for our religious family, which is like a mother to us, and unconditioned respect for its members. This is my legacy, a father's heritage. I entrust this wish to the Sacred Heart of Jesus in the hope that it may be brought to completion through His grace."

[144] Bishop Conforti wrote to the Sacred Congregation for the Evangelization of Peoples.

[145] Luoyang was the first important city in central China to fall under the dominion of the Communists in March 1948. Bishop Bassi served a prison term, and was the last Xaverian missionary to leave China on May 1, 1954. He later worked in Brazil and died in Piacenza, Italy in November 8, 1970, at the age of 93.

[146] Mother Bottego attended a Mission Congress with Fr. Begheldo, s.x. at Notre Dame University, Indiana, from August 26-29th, 1954. She felt perfectly at home in the midst of leading mission experts and members of religious missionary communities. On Sunday August 29th she was present for a meeting of the National Students Mission Crusade. 3000 students from all nations, Africa, China, Indonesia, America. Letter of Mother Bottego to Fr. Spagnolo dated August 26, 1954.

[147] Letter of Mother Bottego August 14, 1954: "Tomorrow at 6:00 a.m. we will see **again** the Statue of Liberty giving us her welcome."

[148] In a letter of Fr. Begheldo to Fr. J. Henry Frassineti dated De-

cember 29, 1954 contained on page 1641 of Documentation vol. X, published Wayne, N.J. 1995-1996 we read: "Upon the arrival of the sisters, some people from various locations organized parties in their honor. The money gathered paid for their voyage. The coming of the sisters made them many friends, and the house has also benefitted from the food and linens which we received as a result. Recently a group of women from Athol – women previously who had no contact with us, nor were they known to us – come every week to the house of the Sisters to do sewing, mending, ironing of our clothes and the linens of the Chapel. Since the coming of these women brought no disciplinary problems to the house, I thought it best to approve of this initiative."

[149] Celestine Bottego left America with her mother for Italy in October 1910. She requested Fr. Bonardi to prepare a passport for her since she wished to make a brief visit to America in a letter dated June 12, 1949. On January 14, 1954 she wrote to the pastor of St Gabriel's Church, Glendale for copies of her baptismal certificate. In this letter she mentioned that she would like to visit her birthplace. When she was at Notre Dame, Indiana, she was within 250 miles from Glendale, Ohio. Mother Bottego did not visit Glendale, Ohio nor Butte, Montana. Rosetta Serra, who was with Mother in the United States, on August 2, 2001 wrote: "I feel bad for not having encouraged Mother to go to Glendale and Butte. At that time I had little experience and we had no money at all. I remember that any small donation we received Mother would sent to San Lazzaro to help build the Motherhouse."

[150] A letter written to Gina, the sister of Maria Grechi.

[151] On June 1951 Pius XII wrote the Encyclical "Evangelii praecones" encouraging mission work in the church, and on April 21, 1957 the same Pius XII called for renewed interest to help the new churches on the African continent.

[152] In a letter to Fr. Spagnolo, dated December 12, 1960, Mother Bottego wrote: "The house in Kiliba is called the House of St Joseph, the Worker. It seems that our friend and protector, St Joseph follows, or rather precedes us everywhere with his invisible presence, and this gives us great courage."

[153] The White Fathers were a missionary congregation founded by Cardinal Charles Lavigierie in Algiers in 1868. About the time of Vatican II the community reverted to use their original name of their foundation "Missionaries of Africa."

[154] Letter to the Missionaries of Mary, dated April 1961.

[155] Letter addressed to the Missionaries of Mary dated April 24, 1963.

[156] Letter addressed to the Missionaries of Mary dated August 29, 1966.

[157] "I met Celestine for the first time in 1948 at the home of Dr. Grossi, a former student of hers. I was immediately and profoundly

struck by her intense spirituality. In 1958 I moved to Rome where I remained for a number of years because of my work. When I returned to Parma, I felt obliged to visit her at San Lazzaro. I was passing through a rather difficult period of my life. She welcomed me in her usual warm way. When I told her that I would like to study music in the quiet of her house, she opened her arms wide as a sign of spontaneous welcome. She told me that her home was at my disposal. I then visited San Lazzaro almost every day to study music and play the piano. She dropped by at times to visit and attentively listened in silence... I went to greet her one day before leaving for Salerno. I had been requested to give a concert there to benefit the work of Padre Pio. The trip was extremely difficult for me. I did not believe that I would be able to make the trip. I went to say goodbye, hopeful perhaps to obtain an additional dose of strength and courage. I was accompanied by some friends, Dr. Grossi and his wife, who were going to travel with me. Once she sensed my preoccupation and concerns, and understood that I could not make the trip alone, she spontaneously offered to travel with me. Her presence sufficed. All proceeded well despite the long voyage..."

[158] Statement by Maestro Paolo Cavazzini, a renowned pianist of Parma who had visited Celestine Bottego at her home over a period of many years. The quotation is taken from the above endnote #157

[159] Mother Bottego was more than aware of "other churches" and mentions them in her writings. "The sisters (in Japan) will attend a school in Kobe... they will find themselves among many other missionaries, some of these are protestant." (Sept. 20, 1960) "These days at Antwerp, Belgium, have been intense and I had various experiences, the meeting with the sisters, an awareness of the missionary environment of their studies and residence, conferences with protestants who work for the unity of the churches." (Apr. 4, 1960) "It is my wish for 1963 that this be an ecumenical year, a year of union, charity and truth with all..." (Jan. 1, 1963)

[160] Statement by Fr. Franco Sottocornola who met Mother Bottego in 1954, and had occasion to meet with her frequently in the sixteen years period during which he taught Liturgy at San Lazzaro.

[161] Address of Mother Bottego given at the inauguration of the Motherhouse of the Missionaries of Mary at San Lazzaro, June 19, 1966.

V

THE FINAL YEARS OF
MOTHER BOTTEGO

1. 1966, a year to look back

Twenty-three years had elapsed since Mother Bottego had been requested to participate in the project of Father Spagnolo. She hesitated. Life moments provides unfulfilled hopes to realize, and its visions are oft viewed through prisms both personal and unique. Her faith, generosity, determination gave voice to her response.

Her "yes," once given, was a leap of faith, an open ended unconditional "self-surrender." New frontiers, challenging horizons, courageous decisions opened before her. She was a "trail-blazer," a "pioneer." However, the protagonist of this resultant foundation was neither she nor Fr. Spagnolo, nor any other. It was the Lord who encouraged and whispered: "It is I, fear not..." and on May 24th 1944 her reply was spoken.

Fr. Spagnolo confessed that he had never thought of founding a community of women religious. Mother Bottego had no aspirations to be a foundress. She had no bag of answers. She was a sower of love seeds. *"Maybe I am called to a spiritual motherhood like Mary."* She was a seeker of truth and a woman "who believed." Perhaps a rhapsody of love was being played between herself and her God. She may have wished to surrender to the Lord of her heart, but she had not yet found the apt concluding note of her solemn and final "Amen."

When Celestine Bottego and Fr. Spagnolo met their individual lives were already quite successful. "Il padre" was a missionary and spiritual guide. "La madre" had been nurtured on Benedictine spirituality and she was a teacher, acclaimed and appreciated. Different though they were, their quest was to be one. Their union grew stronger over the years.[162]

Both "il padre" and "la madre" were chosen by God and entrusted with a singular dream. Theirs was a journey of faith, hope undaunted, and love beyond measure. Together over the years they had sought to give flesh to the dream they lived and realized. "Il padre" and "la madre" moved along side by side in a divine quest. His was a vision clear which needed fine tuning. Hers was a life of faith, engendered hope, and continual concern and love which required direction. Both discovered the hand of God at work in the other so that the Missionaries of Mary might come into being.

On the silver jubilee of Mother Bottego's profession in 1975, Fr. Spagnolo had written : *"Think of the joy we will have together in the Father's house. The Lord brought us together for his work on earth. He will keep us united in his reign. How much more beautiful is our earth when we gaze heavenward! I thank God for this, I thank you who believed my word as the voice of God. Faith makes great things happen. I embrace you spiritually in the Lord."* Their years together in this singular quest demanded a continuous ongoing "give and take" dynamic. They were different and they shared a common vocation.

In 1954 the Xaverian missionaries, along with all other mission groups, in China was forced to leave. These expelled missionaries became part of the Xaverian "post China" diaspora – new missions, new space – in Japan, Indonesia, Bangladesh, Sierra Leone and beyond.

That was the year when the Missionaries of Mary opened their presence in America. In July 1956 two missionaries sisters were lost aboard the Andrea Doria on the evening before they were to arrive in New York. Fr. Spagnolo remarked: *"Look, our community in America opened the way for 'a new presence' in heaven. God's ways are not our own."* Fifteen years later the Missionaries of Mary in America began a priceless apostolate among Hispanic communities in the diocese of Worcester, Mass. The 1974 foundation in Mexico followed and in 1984 a new community was established in Harlem and among Hispanics in upper Manhattan. Language study and professional training has been offered to many missionary sisters now working elsewhere. Mother often used the word "providential", and that is the word which best defines the first foundation outside of Italy by its presence, priorities and ministries.[163]

Other foundations followed. Mother pioneered some, Fr. Spagnolo criss-crossed the world to follow the early years work of the community in Congo, Burundi, Japan, and elsewhere. The family heritage of the Missionaries of Mary had been instilled by Mother Bottego and Fr. Spagnolo. Over the years it was received and treasured as a singular gift to be cherished. It has been ever richly enhanced by the gifts of the Missionaries of Mary themselves and their worldmisssion and continues to be so.

The charism heritage born therefrom is not something staid, rather it is more "ever-readiness." It is not a mere strategy for living. Rather it is a "yes" of open ended service of selfless giving and attentive learning to the Lord who asks for "tutto/all" wherever salvation and hope and love are witnessed and lived, among all nations. The Missionaries of Mary today are a group of dedicated women who believe. Through their faith response they are, have been, and are ever witnesses of God's love, as they sow hope, share a smile, and faith. The Missionaries of Mary were born of a seed mysteriously planted, which experienced and gave testimony to the paschal dying/rising event of Christ, and a future in the "light filled world of Mary."

Mother Bottego's daughters are both religious and missionary. Their faith is real, their obedience prompt, open ended, ready, generous, their love to be enhanced by their outreach to all, and every human need. They are a family of missionaries. Their feminine qualities open doors, and enabled peoples burdened with human trials to find a listening ear, warm welcome, encouraging word and hope. Like Mary, their model, the Missionaries of Mary ponder much in prayerful reflection. Their Marian spirit is Christocentric, they seek Christ and witness Christ wherever they find themselves Their spiritual focus is rooted in the Mercy of God which transformed hearts overcome by sin into life giving witness. God's mercy is tireless, its creative power is abundantly poured forth "to renew the face of the earth."

The bearing buttresses of the spirituality of the Missionaries of Mary, are consecrated religious call, and spontaneous outreach in mission. The Missionaries of Mary wear no special garb. Their habit [164] is the charity with which they work, and the witness to divine love which they give. The arena of their spiritual challenges and combat is mission call, commitment, service. Mother could agree, smile and repeat: *"The Lord alone suffices."*

Today the Missionaries of Mary number some 238, Italian, Brazilian, Japanese, Mexican, Congolese sisters.[165] They work in the Americas; Burundi,[166] Congo, Cameroon-Chad in Africa; Japan and Thailand in Asia. They directed two Polio Homes in Sierra Leone, taught in the schools and assisted in parishes there. On January 25, 1995 seven missionaries were taken hostage by rebel forces for fifty six long days.[167]

2. The First General Chapter of the Missionaries of Mary

On February 1, 1966 Mother Celestine officially announced the dates for the first General Chapter of the Congregation. In the circular letter addressed to the members of her missionary family, she wrote:

"Each sister should give something of her own to the important work of the Chapter. This contribution should be spiritual. It might be a greater effort to live the interior life more fully. Might I suggest that you try to live your faith, hope and love more intensely always, in every occasion which each new day brings.

All that we do is richly enhanced when it is motivated by faith. Actions, imbued by faith are transformed and become greater in God's eyes. Faith which has been tried and tested is all the more genuine.

Hope should endow us with greater confidence and trust in God. It should enable us to trust more readily in our brothers/sisters near at hand. Our thoughts, actions, feelings should be permeated by a profound sense of love so that all may recognize us as disciples of Christ.

A life of faith, hope and love can and will, believe me, be the best preparation for the chapter and enable it to obtain the graces which the congregation needs at this moment.

Ask Mary to teach us to believe, hope and love so that we may receive the grace to deeply appreciate and re-discover the grace of our baptism, so that we, like her, may be malleable instruments in the Lord's hands for the mission with which the Lord has entrusted us."

3. Mother Bottego ceded her directive role

All these events, her early foundations, the Council, the new Motherhouse, Chapter preparations, brought her to another moment of decision. During this first General Chapter in 1966 Mother Celestine unexpectedly resigned as Directress General. She accompanied her gesture with a letter which reveals the finesse of her maternal heart and her keen understanding of the biblical expression "useless servant." These words portray the reality she had lived, acquired and by which she had been guided for long years.

Her letter of resignation is dated September 24th, 1966: *"My dearly beloved sisters, the first General Chapter marks the conclusion of our first twenty years together. I sincerely thank each of you individually for all that you have done for the society and me, and for the gift of yourselves. God knows how to repay you, I hope that you find some consolation in the decisions taken at this first General Chapter. These may be seen as a compendium of all that we have together accomplished.*

Now I wish to sing my 'Nunc dimittis,' and offer my contribution to our work, in prayer, service and simply as 'mother'.[168]

129

You can well understand as time goes on, how our work demands ever new and fresh energy and youthful gifts to respond to new challenges. Our work is moving forward, and it cannot slow its pace. I wish to withdraw, better observe and follow the activity of all of you, my daughters, and proffer spiritual assistance.

At the beginning of our work, as you well know, I hesitated much before accepting the invitation of 'il padre.' I knew that I did not have the requisite gifts for such a committed work. My 'yes' was given to assist 'il padre' begin until the time when others would be prepared to substitute me. Things have proceeded in ways quite different from what I could have foreseen. However, the idea to cede my role has ever remained alive. I believe that the Lord wants to take this responsibility from me now, and I voluntarily yield this role to you, my daughters.

I feel obliged to humbly ask pardon, first of God and then of you, who represent all of my daughters. Notwithstanding my weaknesses and faults, you know that in my heart I cherish great love for each of you and a very ardent desire to give you to Jesus in others. Let us be prepared with great faith, vibrant hope and ardent love to accept all and whatever the Chapter will present as the expressions of the will of God. Let us pray insistently to Our Lady that she may remain in our midst, as she did with the apostles, with her love and powerful maternal intercession. Mother Celestine Bottego."

The full impact of this decision and what inspired it is best understood in due perspective. The decision flows from her life of faith lived in obedience to the will of God. Commentaries of this decisive gesture cannot adequately comprehend her clear choice which had matured over long years in the fertile earth of her soul, and in prayerful reflection with her God. Her "resignation" finds meaning only in God's will.[169] Mother Celestine stepped out of the administrative scene to be Mother only, and by so doing her voice regarding the community she founded and "Villa Bottego," her family home, would now be more silent. Here we can discover a touch of the "tut-to/all" and of a following uncommon. Time has revealed the greatness and true significance of the unexpected declaration of Mother Bottego to the first General Chapter of the Missionaries of Mary.[170]

In faith she had accepted her directive role, and in faith did she consign it back to her daughters and step aside. Her new role was one that she cherished.

4. Simply Mother

In 1966 the direction of the Institute passed to a new Directress General and her council. Mother Bottego, then, took on a role which was singularly hers and hers alone, that of "Mother." She was quite discreet, she progressively withdrew from the active life of the congregation. She dedicated herself almost completely to prayer and correspondence. She remembered her daughters, near and those in faraway lands. She welcomed her missionaries when they returned to the mother house, and followed them affectionately when they departed anew. She was present at the joyful and sad moments of the community. These were activities which filled her usual routine. She penned thousands of letters, and her messages were heart sent. These maternal caring notes bear witness to her boundless love which constantly continued to provide life-giving lymph for the "family." Mother underwent a delicate operation for a hiatal hernia, and she tired easily as a result. Physical and spiritual trials and moments of concern were not lacking, as they had not been absent throughout the earlier history of the "Missionaries of Mary."

"Mother" was her title, not a privilege nor prerogative, it was a role of service. She had noble traits and she ably dealt with the humble and the great with like availability and simplicity. She never feared the presence of others, she was elated by the good which she witnessed and

131

could stimulate around her. She never descended to the mediocre, wanted no part in power games nor privileges. Magnanimous was she, and ever ready to forgive and excuse.

Her days were full, her motherly concerns many. Her daughters, wherever they might be, continued to be her care. She showed interest in what they were doing, in all that they had accomplished. Her conversations made her presence felt, her letters, always personal, enabled her to be with her daughters. She was "Mother" and, ever concerned that her missionaries succeeded in what they were about. Their successes were in some small way her successes, and their spiritual growth enabled her to thank the Lord for the gifts which each possessed and represented.

Friendship was a characteristic quality which she prized and treasured. Her caring notes were addressed to her daughters, longtime friends, acquaintances. Her pen reached out to embrace those dear to her, and to offer encouragement, an uplifting word, and a sense of true presence. Each word was written to be received as "gift," and each message etched upon a heart with a smile contained a subtle invitation to higher things.

She was a person who could see far beyond the present to new tomorrows. Her care, affection, and communications were open ended. She recognized the value of prayer and she wrote to numberless monastic communities requesting their members to accompany her missionaries with prayer and sacrifice. She recalled the monastic discipline of cloistered nuns and remind her own missionaries that their cloister was to be found elsewhere in the arena of mission, the world, and family.

She was concerned that work and activity be carried out within due boundaries, lest the important time for prayer suffer. She spoke of unity, charity, and imparted self esteem, acceptance of others. She was for the "family" and its members all.[171]

She had been warned that a religious must be ready

to be a "dust rag," she mindfully adapted to different tasks, roles, situations. She knew where the buck stopped, and she could be in charge and walk along roads less trodden. She was "Mother." Her mother had taught her by example how to listen to learn from her daughters. Her years as a teacher had taught her to be an attentive learner if she hoped to teach well.

5. Her letters provided a guiding hand

Mother Celestine penned forty-two circular letters. They allowed her to get caught up, when work, travel, health caused her to fall behind.

Letters were, for her, a powerful way to create community spirit. Common letters assured all that the sisters were followed, their letters appreciated, valued, attentively read and kept close. Her letters transmitted news, reports about construction projects, benefactors and their needs, anniversaries, and information about church documents and Vatican II council suggestions. Her letters were often peppered with brief oft repeated spiritual and practical reflections. The following are some "snippets" from these common letters.

"Leave a little margin to Almighty God."

"Love is the motive force of our consecrated life, and prayer its powerhouse."

"Put your trust and anchor in the Lord, who is ever faithful and stands firm."

"We are vital cells in the body of community, hence we are to be perfect in action, word, thought."

"Life is brief, we are to live it to the fullest lovingly."

"Charity for others suffices not, until our love is pure, vibrant, active like the love Jesus has for us."

"Christian perfection is attained not until a love for the hidden life, humiliations and opposition is acquired." [172]

"Charity is not great deeds alone. Unity and community are possible and perfected in small deeds and ways."

" Joy and happiness are constants of the religious life."
(Pius XII)
"I wish to be good with all at any cost."
(Blessed John XXIII)
"A good sense of humor resolves many problems."
(Mother Mary Joseph, Maryknoll Sisters' foundress)

St. Therese reminds us that *"we will be judged by love."* Mother Celestine added: *"How true this saying with the passage of years. Therese's little way is an invitation to love, sacrifice and silence."*

"Smile a while, and while you smile, another smiles and soon there's miles and miles and life's worth while because you smile!" [173]

She was "mother." She praised and encouraged her daughters for their generous service, dedication, and for "having believed."

She recognized life's seasons, the boundless potential experienced in the early of the Missionaries of Mary. *"The enthusiasm of beginnings, often presents all things as possible, and engenders generous responses to edge forward and attain the goal. Mission and the apostolate have greater appeal and command even greater committed responses..."*

November was a time to celebrate deceased loved ones. Thanksgiving focused on personal giftedness and gratitude for every gift received from God and so many others.

In January 1963 Mother Celestine offered a program for the future. She wrote of new openings, a better preparation of the sisters in the future. She reminded the community: *"If time is money, as the adage goes, use it well."* Time was a precious commodity to win souls for God and witness God's love. She proposed the spiritual and corporal works of mercy as the focus for the year and she closed her letter by citing these works: *"Blessed are the merciful! Instruct the ignorant, counsel the doubtful, admonish sinners, bear wrongs patiently, forgive offenses, comfort the afflicted, pray for the living and the dead."* The corporal works were also listed: *"Feed the hungry, give*

134

*drink to the thirsty, clothe the naked, shelter the homeless, visit the sick, ransom the captive, bury the dead... **for they will obtain mercy!**" (Mt 5,7)*

6. Villa Bottego, her home, where memories dwelt

Mother Bottego loved her home, the grounds of her family "Villa." Re-zoning within the city of Parma in the 1970 took away the stately tree lined road which led up to the residence.[174] Memories remained nonetheless. A solitary grapevine which bordered a dirt path and had survived now wanders along aimlessly. The nut trees which her father, John (Battista) had planted years earlier provide welcome shade. The land teaches many lessons about life such as the axiom. "The deeper a tree sinks its roots into the earth the greater are the chances of growing and producing fruit." [175] The land in San Lazzaro spoke of family remembrances, friendship encounters, and a stroll of Celestine through the property, with one or another of her daughters, memories all.

Mother Bottego was polite, simple and noble in her manner, and both strong and caring in her way of loving. Even in her later years, when her strength waned with advancing age, she retained her peaceful and profound dignified manner which ever commanded due respect. This was not the only aspect which touched those who, with mixed feelings of both admiration and affection, came into contact with her. She reserved within herself a secret place, the world where she habitually dwelt, and which served as her true abode alone with God.

Mother walked the familiar paths of her property in every season with Lavinia, her faithful companion in her later years. They sowed the prayers of the rosary, recalled missionary family members, and imbibed the lessons which country living provides.

Mother was quick to recount tales of the past, and to describe the unique beauty of each changing season, varied trees, plants, crops. She contemplated nature, read seasonal signs, and found her God therein. Her ears listened for the song of the birds, and chirping crickets. The passing of each season retold the tale of a cycle of life and death, and new life beginning. The month of May presented the endless dance of the grain interacting with the singular bright red poppies scattered here and there. The freshly plowed earth of autumn spoke of new harvests. The sun haphazardly focused its brilliant rays on the yellow and rose leaves of the vineyard.

Mother was an avid reader of nature and its changing seasons and she found reason to rejoice and be grateful always. She welcomed the heavy winter fog, the biting cold which stripped the trees of their foliage. Every season had its own beauty and message. From her room, warmed by the afternoon sun, on the third floor south she could view the Apennines, the Bottego outer lands, and recall lifelong friendships and past happenings. Villa Bottego had always been her home since 1910 when she arrived, a young lady endowed with rich dreams from Butte, Montana. Whenever she strolled or wherever she looked she spontaneously witnessed the signature of an ever loving present God.[176]

7. Mother's vocation journey in "her own words"

With her resignation Mother Bottego began a new chapter in her life. Her vocation story had many moments as well. As she penned her loving missives and short notes, she remembered occurrences and her own vocation story. The following slightly adapted quotations describe her vocation journey "in her own words."

"The thought of a religious vocation is persistent and ever present." (Butte, Montana 1910)

"My early confessors in Italy told me that I had a vocation, and that I should give due consideration to this." (December 1972, remembrance)

"Maria did well (to enter the convent). I tell myself this everyday. Her life is now more full. Whenever I think of her, I feel obliged to be better." (January 20th, 1924, a letter)

"I like teaching, it keeps me on my toes. It puts me in contact with so many young people... This is not life, this is merely an accommodation. I have a lot of energy, and I would like to live more intensely for a single goal." (letter to Luisa Bulleri 1928)

"I do not feel the absence of physical motherhood, perhaps I am called to a spiritual motherhood like Mary." (A letter dated Parma, 1931) [177]

"A nurse's diploma may permit me to work with my sister in India." (A letter dated Parma 1932)

"The fields (in India) are ripe for the harvest, why do so very few respond? Love is lacking. We ought to pray that we might be less unworthy instruments to make Jesus Christ known." (From an article in Le Missioni illustrate, June 1937)

"I am more able to destroy than build the works of the Lord." (Reply given to Fr. Spagnolo's project)

"On your Easter card you wrote a sublime word on which I have meditated." (Reply to the Easter card of Fr. Spagnolo)

"Could my negative response have been dictated by an attachment to a comfortable life?" (May 24, 1944)

"I followed your advice. I spoke to my confessor about my decision. He thought I was too old and lacking in requisite qualities for the religious life. I told him that the voice was clear and I thought it would be an offense to delay any longer and oblige the Lord to wait. If this proves to be a mere personal illusion, and not the will of God, I am sure that I could leave it quite easily. It would cost me little." (Letter to Fr. Spagnolo dated February 21, 1945)

"That I am now engaged in this work seems to be a dream. For a long time I resisted the religious life. I was convinced that I was not called. Then all at once I perceived an unexpected light, which changed my soul and mind, and helped me understand the beauty of this life.

There was such a radical change within me after that. I had no doubt whatsoever that what occurred was an expression of the will of God." (Letter of Mother Bottego to Fr. Turci dated November 1946)

"Ten years ago today I met my sister again in Hyderabad after nine years of separation. Lord, how many changes have you brought about in my life through your goodness and through no merit of my own. Since then you have been preparing my 'path.' I can repeat with my sister: 'Since then the 'way' has been becoming more determined and the goal more bright and clear'." (From her diary, August 16, 1946)

"I was together with the sisters who renewed their vows. I don't believe I ever experienced more the beauty of our consecration and the joy of repeating my 'yes' to the Lord with such understanding."[178] (Letter dated March 28, 1954)

"With the sisters we meditated on the word 'yes' by which we replied to the Lord when called to the religious life. Ten years ago I did not fully understand the commitment which I was assuming. Today I believe that I am better aware of that call and I wish to be faithful in responding to every expression of the will of God. For some time now Jesus is teaching me the importance of being docile to the one who represents him." (Letter dated May 24, 1954)

"I seemed to relive the first days of my encounter with 'il padre.' In an atmosphere of pure faith and great fervor I said 'yes' to a persistent inner drive which I could not resist. I knew I was free, yet I was not free. I count on your prayers, it is so easy to ruin the work of God by lacking in charity and humility toward those near at hand and who are entrusted to me."[179] (May 24, 1954)

"At the beginning I hesitated before accepting. I did not have the requisite gifts. My 'yes' was given to help Father get started, until others would be prepared. Things proceeded quite differently. The idea to give up my role has ever been alive in me. The Lord wants to take this responsibility from me. I voluntarily yield this role to my daughters.

I wish to sing my 'Nunc dimittis' (now, you may let your servant go in peace), and offer my contribution simply as 'mother'." (September 24, 1966 resignation statement)

"This date marks the 25ᵗʰ anniversary of our foundation. Pray that we may preserve the spirit of faith which inspired the generosity and zeal of the first sisters, and the spirit of charity which enabled them to overcome our initial difficulties, with great simplicity and serenity. Let us thank the Lord. For you, I ask the grace to be able to generously and simply give your "yes" to every thing the Lord asks of you through the voice of the Pope and your superiors. The acts of faith, hope and love, which our obedience expects of us, will increase the grace in each of us and in our religious family." (May 24ᵗʰ, 1969)

"Thanks for everything you do. I ask pardon for everything. Let us seek whatever the Lord wants from us. I bless you. Thank you for everything. Here I am. Amen." (Words spoken on her death bed, August 1980)

8. Fr. Spagnolo, his last years

Fr. Spagnolo was diagnosed with a malignant tumor in the spring of 1977. He visited Lourdes in February 1978, on the 120ᵗʰ anniversary of the first apparition to Bernardette. He wrote: *"The greatest grace is not 'to remain' but to successfully attain one's goal. The closer we are to our final goal, the clearer things become. The time remaining ought to be joyful, it is a festive preparation for the great encounter."* He made the sentiments of Ps 131 his own: *"I have stilled and quieted my soul like a weaned child, like a weaned child in its mother's lap so is my soul within me."*[180]

Mother Celestine followed the illness of Fr. Spagnolo closely. She silently followed him through the various stages of his illness, final days, and self oblation. Her concern for him was such that she overlooked the gravity of her own critical health condition. Fr. Giacomo

Spagnolo was "homeward bound," and his joy was full. Mother Bottego had still to wait before she attained the goal and fullness of her own life.

Fr. Giacomo Spagnolo died at 7:20 a.m. on the Wednesday of Holy Week, March 22, 1978 while the missionaries of the Motherhouse community were at Mass. During the liturgy of Holy Thursday at San Lazzaro, Bishop Gianni Gazza [181] commemorated important moments of the life of Fr. Giacomo Spagnolo. The funeral of Fr. Giacomo Spagnolo took place in the chapel of the Xaverian missionaries on Good Friday. The Missionaries of Mary, his beloved daughters, and numerous Xaverian fathers, relatives, and many friends were present. Fr. Gabriel Ferrari, Superior General of the Xaverian missionaries presided at the liturgy and funeral service.[182]

Shortly before his death Fr. Giacomo addressed a final circular letter to his missionaries. It was pre-dated Easter 1978.[183] On that same Easter Sunday, March 26, 1978, four days after the death of Fr. Giacomo, Mother Celestine wrote her final circular letter to her beloved daughters: *"For us this is a time of deep sorrow, a time of detachment from 'il padre.' I firmly believe that this is a gifted time, a moment of grace. 'Il padre' will now reveal God's thoughts to us more clearly. We will be able to comprehend and be taken up into a higher reality, about which he often spoke and desired to happen. No longer do we speak to him as a mortal, but we look to his spirit which reflects the gifts which God wants to bestow on this 'work.' I remember 'il padre' and I believe that conversation with him will be easier, more profound, and fruitful. During his life 'il padre' gave as much of himself as was possible. Now, he is with God, and he possesses and can share a much fuller reality, to encourage and sanctify us, that we may be capable of loving. I feel you all gathered around 'il padre' who awaits us in heaven. I embrace you with all of the tenderness of my heart."*

9. Mother Celestine in the sunset of her life

After the death of Fr. Spagnolo, Mother Bottego's role as foundress was re-dimensioned. She did not pull in her oars nor lower her sails. On the contrary she generously poured out all that she still possessed as a final libation that her offering might be complete, total, pure, pleasing. Mother Bottego considered her approaching death and detachment as a preparatory stage of the paschal mystery, which she and Fr. Spagnolo had lived, shared and experienced together during their lifetimes.

A post Vatican Council document [184] "Ecclesiae Sanctae", issued on August 6, 1966 mandated that every religious community should re-examine, re-elaborate, update and relaunch its proper constitutions in fidelity to church guidelines, and the original charism of the founders. The unexpected death of Fr. Giacomo Spagnolo, founder, left a void among the Missionaries of Mary. The third General Chapter of the Congregation, held in 1978, was entrusted with reformulating the constitutions. Paradoxically, the absence of Fr. Spagnolo stimulated and permitted the chapter participants to themselves discover a more authentic, responsible declaration of their charism and heritage. Recognizing that this was not a simple task, Mother Celestine accompanied this delicate work of her daughters with a determination admirable for a person of her age and physical stamina. Mother was present at various sessions of the General Chapter and she showed her interest in developments taking place around the world.

Mother Celestine's life was a parable of faith. As the years passed and she sensed the end drawing near, Mother, with a clear, determined voice and joyful readiness, intoned her own "Nunc dimittis." "Now, Master, you can dismiss your servant in peace." With a masterful hand Luke portrays a god-fearing and just man, Simeon, who prophesied about the Savior and intoned his "Nunc dimittis." His heart is where his treasure rests, and he is anxious to arrive home. His heart dances, his eyes, shadowed by the light of this world, are wide open to a new light come to illumine his path and call the nations home.

She did so with her customary naturalness and nobility. From our human vantage point we can identify a number of the recurrent constants which were ever present throughout her lifetime. Fearlessness and meekness, generosity and moderation, respect and simplicity, authority and service, all harmoniously meld together to enhance her rich life. Artists attain mastery and perfection through the persistent use of their skills and talents, Mother Bottego's traits appear co-natural and they are evidenced in all phases of her long life. Her final goal in life was firmly set, and nothing deflected her attention from arriving to that firmly established goal.

Her gifts were numerous, her character strong, her faith indomitable. Mother Celestine could temper her innate ability to teach, counsel and guide, with humility, meekness, and joy. She was open to the new, her intelligence was vital and keen, she sought not words of praise or places of honor. In Montana her family was adequately provided for, in Italy she lived her adult life in an upper social class home. Despite the family wealth, good standing, a comfortable life, she was able to share the lot of the less fortunate, opt for a life of following her Master, who was meek and humble of heart.

Mother Celestine accepted the final years of her life in silence and faith, with the customary attitudes and personal traits which she had acquired and made her own. "Now it is time to dismiss your servant," she had experienced much, known joy and suffering, and kept many things locked within her heart. Her serenity, faith rooted, persevered. However, she was as serene and aware as she had been throughout the years, however his illness drained her strength and left her tired more often. The time had arrived for her to engage and encounter the paschal mystery in its fullest realization. She prepared to let go of all remaining earthly ties.

Like her Model, Mary, Mother Celestine was a woman of faith. She was humble, a real woman in the fullest sense of the word. Celestine emulated the maternal solicitude which Our Lady had for all, especially the weakest and the poorest. Her heart was the sanctuary within which she reflected on events, her call, and destiny, while awaiting and trusting in the now time, the "hour" of God.

She knew how to be a woman and mother, in the ordinary etymological sense of the word of "domina" or "signora" or "lady." She was mother in the true sense of the word, she was a life giver in the Lord's plan. She never renounced the gifts which enhanced her rich humanity, nor did she put aside her feminine finesse. She walked a balanced path where the spiritual thrived and conventional wisdom had its proper place. The limpid streams of the word of God and the bread of life nurtured the inner freedom which she possessed.

Her "Nunc dimittis" provides a wonderful rendition with due variations of the single theme omnipresent throughout her life. Her "be it done to me" was her unconditioned and total response to the Lord who asked her for "tutto/all."

10. The subtle melody of the paschal mystery

The paschal mystery provided a background accompaniment for the life of Mother Celestine. It was ever there, more so however, in her latter years. It seemed to be pruning season once more. Mother Maria Giovanna, her sister, who returned home to Italy [185] after forty two years of uninterrupted missionary service in India, had died on January 30th, 1970. Mother Celestine's brother Vittorio died unexpectedly two years later.[186] She was now sole survivor and heir of an exceptional family which had expended the best of itself in adventure, explorations and especially missionary life. Mother Celestine accepted and considered this last period of her life as providential, she was grateful for the diverse fecundity which the plan of God gave to her family and herself in the now established world family of numerous daughters, the Missionaries of Mary. At the end of 1977, during the final illness of Fr. Spagnolo, Mother Bottego was diagnosed with breast cancer and she underwent surgery on February 18th, 1978.

After her surgery in February, 1978, her physicians were concerned for her health. Metastasis was feared and it soon manifested its presence. Mother Celestine realized that she tired more easily, and her strength waned. Her body progressively grew weaker. At times she had to spend whole days in bed. However, when the afternoon sun warmly filled her third floor room, she was never without her proverbial smile. She extended her open arms wide, as was her custom, to receive visitors. In June 1980, following the advice of her doctors, she underwent further surgery and therapy to no avail. This intervention had a negative effect on her general physical condition.

In August 1980 Mother Bottego was admitted to the Stuard Hospital of Parma. Perhaps because of the meager results of the treatment, or more likely due to her insistence to be at home, she returned to "Villa Bottego." Parma suffered a very severe heat wave that year, the air was heavy and still. Breathing was quite difficult especially for the seriously ill. The city was silent. The streets were deserted. Fields across the road from the "Villa" were dry and burnt by the sun. The summer heat had reached its peak, there was little breeze and no relief.

Mother Bottego had a room on the north side of the house where it was a bit cooler and more quiet. From the open windows, she could hear the crickets sing and sparrows chirp as they moved from one branch to another. At that time of the year many sisters were away from San Lazzaro for summer activities. When the serious condition of Mother Celestine became known, they anticipated their return. The Motherhouse was usually a very busy place. Now it was silent and prayerful. It was a time for waiting. Missionary sisters tiptoed about, spoke in hushed whispers to disturb as little as possible.

Notwithstanding her weakened condition, Mother Celestine received everyone with kindness and gratitude. During her final days she often repeated *"Let us pray... pray... "* *"Thanks for all you do for me..."* Attentive to others more than to herself, when she woke up she would ask: *"I slept... did you? Go and rest."* Aware the end was near, one of her missionary daughters asked if she was suffering much, she replied: *"The Lord knows... just think I don't know what is happening to me... I ask pardon for everything... I am close to the end."*

She was very tired, her words were often incomplete, then she told those who were assisting her: **"Let us seek to be a 'part,' my dearest ones... it is hard, it is difficult. In any way we are all desirous to go ahead... Let us always seek whatever the Lord wants from us. I bless you... I bless all of you... Thank you, thank you, thank you for everything."**[187]

The 18th of August was a particularly difficult day for Mother Celestine. In the afternoon she wanted to see some elderly guests of the house and with great affection she asked them about "her missionaries." Bishop Gazza, who grew up very close to "Villa Bottego" visited Mother and he brought greetings from all the Xaverian missionaries and he imparted absolution and a special blessing.

On the next day she had trouble breathing. She repeated: *"Yes... yes..."* and then *"here I am... here I am."* At 4:30 in the afternoon Bishop Gazza celebrated the Eucharist in her room with all of the community members present. During Mass he administered the sacrament of the sick. At communion time, she made a gesture symbolic of her life. She opened her arms wide in her usual way of welcome and greeting and with a clear voice and a serene countenance she voiced a solemn **"Amen"** which, for its force and intensity, remained impressed on all present.

During the night, she rested but toward midnight she took a turn for the worst and expired a few minutes later. It was August 20th. She was eighty-four years and eight months old.

"During her life 'la madre' gave as much of herself as possible.

Now, she is with God, and she shares a much fuller reality, to encourage and sanctify you, that you may be capable of loving.

With padre, – I, la madre – await you in heaven to embrace you with all of the tenderness of my heart." (Paraphrase of Mother's note written on the occasion of Fr. Spagnolo's death applied to her own passing).

12. Final farewells

Her body was prepared, for the wake which was held in the chapel of the Motherhouse of the Missionaries of Mary. On the morning of August 20th, Mons. Gazza celebrated Mass in a very familial manner in the community chapel with the sisters gathered around her coffin. It was not sorrow, but gratitude to God for the gift of a person like Mother Bottego which permeated the hearts all those present. He continued his remarks and focused on Mother whom he had known since his early childhood and said: "I don't ever remember having seen a frown, or any shadows on her countenance, her presence always reflected her customary and usual traits and coherence with the Gospel."

Once the news of her death became known in Parma, a continuous uninterrupted line of people came to pause and pray by her body, even though August was the time of the summer exodus from the city.

On August 22nd the Missionaries of Mary gathered in their chapel at San Lazzaro for a moving and fitting family farewell before the official ceremony in the Cathedral. Bishop Gazza presided and spoke at this ceremony: "The woman whom you call Madre, the Mother of this, your missionary family, leaves this home where she lived all of

146

her life. Mother came here from the United States when she was fifteen. For seventy years she lived here.[188] Here she grew and matured, here the whole story of her life was acted out. The outcome, goal, accomplishments of her life were unforeseeable.

This house served as the heartbeat of the population which lives hereabout. Is there anyone in San Lazzaro who did not know the signorina Bottego? Her life unfolded here and her consecration matured gradually. Our impressions and remembrances of her remain unchanged. I knew her for fifty years, for me Mother Celestine today is the Signorina Bottego of yesterday. From this house where her religious life matured, she generously sowed treasures of her heart through her charity.

Although she was raised in a well to do family, Mother Bottego was at the service of all. The family home grew in size. Signorina Bottego became Mother Bottego. Mother, in her this title is so singular, so meaningful, – one might say – so apt, appropriate, and fitting. When she gave birth to the Missionaries of Mary, her motherhood truly became great, as great as the world.

Here in this house Mother brought her human existence and activities to a close. She died as she had lived. During these days of my presence in your midst, I experienced the climate of her serenity, faith, love. This is the treasured heritage of your Mother who has left you. In her heritage you can discover the faith for which she lived, through which she created this Institute for the missions, and for which she gave her life."

Parma celebrated "one of its own." At the end of the simple rite in San Lazzaro on the morning of August 22nd, the funeral procession, preceded by a motorcycle escort, made its way to the Cathedral where a numerous crowd of people were gathered, among with the many religious and priests.

Her daughters carried the coffin of Mother Bottego down the central nave of the Duomo. Numerous simple folk reached out from the crowd to touch or kiss the cof-

147

fin as a final sign of farewell. These were simple, humble, faith inspired acts, which were gestures and signs of appreciation, respectful gratitude, and sincere thanks expressive of times far beyond the present moment.

The city and the diocese of Parma united to acknowledge their common loss and to accompany Mother to her final resting place, with the customary greeting: "addio/go to God." Mons. Amilcare Pasini, Bishop of Parma presided over the solemn concelebration and assembly.[189] The participants in the Eucharistic celebration gave ample witness to a life humbly lived in selfless altruistic service and a motherhood which reached out to embrace the world.

The gospel repeated the beatitudes. Bishop Pasini reflected on life of Mother Bottego: "*Whenever I encountered Mother Celestine Bottego I was always left with the same impression. She was a happy person, a soul radiating trust, a woman of boundless serenity. Her heart challenged others to love Jesus in our brothers and sisters. Always! She lived the Gospel beatitudes to the fullest. Whenever we met I was always edified and filled with admiration for her. She was magnanimous in all her ways, her appearance, her personality, her gestures. Yet she could and did become small, humble before all. She loved the phrase: 'Learn from me for I am meek and humble of heart.' She made an expression of Blessed Conforti her own: 'If you wish to do good, be meek; if you want to do more, be even more meek; if you want to do even greater good, be meek without limits.' Mother Celestine was such always!*"

After the final blessing, to the words of the hymn, "I believe that I will rise..." the coffin of Mother Celestine was carried by her daughters for the last time through the crowded nave of the cathedral to the waiting hearse. The long funeral procession solemnly passed through the streets and various neighborhoods of Parma on its way to the cemetery. Thus the whole city was able to bid adieu to one of its own. The body of Mother Bottego rests in the family tomb with her parents, her sister, Mother

Maria Giovanna, her brother, Vittorio and the first of her deceased missionary daughters.

Not far away is the tomb of Fr. Giacomo Spagnolo. Together "il padre" and "la madre" continue to bless and guide their missionary family on many continents throughout the world. New members, from many nations, have come to crown a motherhood and a fatherhood which are rooted and have reason to be in that kingdom in which "every tongue will sing the glory of the Lord."

12. Their memory will be ever blessed (Sir 46,11)

People who met Mother Celestine for the first time were impressed by her smile and serenity. She was stately, tall, heavy set, imposing yet her maternal manner enabled all to feel at home in her presence. The Italian features of her father and the Irish-American countenance of her mother enhanced her noble appearance. Her face was oval, her features clear, and she had an easy smile, a ready Irish wit, and interior peace. Her blue eyes were clear and serene, yet they could at times become serious and reflective as if an inner voice and presence were calling her elsewhere.

The Cavazzini family had lived in Villa Bottego at one time. Franco and Sr. Vittoria recall: *"Celestine held me in her arms from my earliest days, she accompanied me as I grew. I defined our relationship as 'a heavenly contact.' I experienced her serenity during my entire life. When Celestine died, it seemed as thought I had lost my second mother. I visited her a few days before she died. She was drowsy, her eyes were closed. She seemed far away, silent, lost in her thoughts. I told her that I wished her well. When she heard my voice, she opened her eyes, embraced and kissed me. Then she said: 'Yes, I know Franco wishes me well,' and she closed her eyes and drifted away once more."*[190]

"She was so close to all of us. She was always serene.

*She was a woman of peace. She accompanied me in my
life as a religious. She was present in all of the various circumstances of the life of our family."* [191]

Countless are those people who experienced the
warmth and tenderness of Mother Celestine first hand.
Her affection, motherly love, sisterly concern revealed
sincere friendship, abundant goodness, and imparted joy.
She was a Missionary of Mary, and Mary became her
Model and guide. She observed, pondered, learned and
then taught by her presence, example, written and spoken word.

All of Mother Bottego's circular letters are sprinkled
with expressions of her affection for Our Lady. In her letter, which was addressed to her Missionaries of Mary
(May 11, 1965) she offered some insights regarding Marian devotion. *"During the month of May we are once again
spiritually gathered with our Mother Mary. Consider for a
moment, the inner world of Our Lady and contrast it with
the world that the evil one presents to us at times. We must
have clear ideas about both worlds, that we may be able to
make prompt and clear choices.*

*Mary's month is a time of re-commitment and imita-
tion of our Lady's example. Mother's day provides an invitation to show filial affection to earthly mothers.*

*The world of Mary is filled with light and simplicity. In
that world one lives by faith, love, hope and peace even in
time of sorrow. A person who lives in this world, as Mary,
our Blessed Mother did, is strong, serene, patient, meek in
the midst of the contrarieties of life. Like Mary, such a person suffers in silence, forgives in the depths of our heart,
and everywhere sows peace and joy since she does not seek
herself. She knows how to be patient and wait for others,
understand them, excuse, console and maternally encourage.*

*This is the world that we, Missionaries of Mary, have
chosen. Our Lady will remain close to us to help us in our
lifelong struggle. Through victories attained you will possess much clarity, light, and simplicity for your life. I am*

150

maternally close, I follow you in your experiences and successes."

Mother Celestine lived this choice of Mary's world throughout her entire life. Mother found herself one with Mary on the road of mystery and faith, from the annunciation's "fiat" to the profound silence of Calvary's "it is consummated." In Mary, the woman, virgin, mother, Celestine discovered the way to reach Christ and to proclaim him, in turn, to the world in full coherence with her own femininity and motherhood.

"Missionary of Mary" is the title which best describes the personality and spirituality of Mother Bottego. From her "fiat/be it done" at Capriglio to the solemn "amen" pronounced shortly before her death, her identity with Mary was total and complete. It would not be out of place to compare her life to a rosary in which the joyful, sorrowful, glorious mysteries once more scanned the whole world in her living.

Devotion to Our Lady is a constant in Mother Bottego's life, it is present in almost all of her correspondence. It reveals how generously and faithfully she accepted the missionary ideal of Fr. Spagnolo, her own.[192]

In 1969 Fr. Spagnolo offered a brief description of this characteristic Marian, religious, mission spirit. *"To experience, like Mary did, the Paschal mystery of Christ is to spiritually live the life of heaven on earth, as Mary did. Totally similar to Christ, Our Lady fulfilled in herself that which St Paul says: 'If you would rise with Christ, seek and taste the things above, and not those of earth.' This means that we are to live and share in the paschal mystery of Christ with the spiritual attitude and orientations of Mary."*

Mother Celestine made this ideal her very own. She lived it totally, and she made it credible and attainable for others. For Mother Bottego Mary was the woman par excellence, and Mother Celestine knew how to make her own femininity a canticle, and her motherhood a gift which continually gives life to the church and the world.

Mother Bottego lived a full life. Mother Celestine

lived in the new and old worlds, witnessed two world wars – experienced hostage taking, bombings, hostile war time occupation, partisan guerrilla clashes, food shortages, summary executions, shattered dreams, simple beginnings – through it all her smile was proverbial. That smile was her i.d. card. Farm workers sought their rights, she identified with their cause. Future opportunities for the children of San Lazzaro were limited, possibilities less, her doors and heart opened wide to them and she sowed hope. Socialism and anticlericalism raised their voices, her life as catechesis witnessed and proclaimed faith in a caring, compassionate God. Her unassuming manner won hearts, and her presence helped the impossible become possible.

Her life story recalls Ireland's potato blight, Butte miners' plight, worker rights, a Congo mission flight, a new found Burundi site. Her maternal touch was everywhere felt, the Andrea Doria loss strained her loving heart, India had enkindled her mission dreams. The blight, plight, flight, new site, losses and dreams found meaning as she pondered all, like Mary her model, before the Lord in her heart. Life's events were numerous, her focus singular, continuous, intense, she sought the Lord.

Her eyes made friends of people. Her heart beat with compassion and loving concern. She was the "signorina." She was the 'sjorén`na.' She was the "professoressa." She was the significant figure of the neighborhood of San Lazzaro, a special person called, chosen, sent, a witness of serenity, joy, human solidarity, affection. Childless she was not, she embraced the world and her goodness and dreams persist and live on in those who call her "Mother" and were touched by her maternal embrace.

From the "gallows" of Butte, Montana to a Velasquez crucifixion image, from a persistent voice on a retreat day in 1910 to the hamlet of Capriglio's unconditioned response she made her way home, one step at a time, resolutely, giving "all" and attaining "her all," God alone.

152

Her eyes embraced human need in Italy, Bombay, Kashmir, along India's rivers and mountains, aboard ship, in Dakar, Congo, Burundi, Brazil, and even in tiny Petersham, Massachusetts, and she could not turn away or refuse a response.

Every event, each page in a life story is significant. Her life journal was marked by her constant thirst for learning, and her proffered "how to" solutions. Mining camp beginnings, European schooling, "Villa Bottego" upbringing, a welcoming homestead, all provide memories of what had been and was yet unfolding. The foundation of the Missionaries of Mary continues to transform her family home into an international oasis where mission quest and a world service mandate have been and are well written.

Her scant eighty-five years provide a cameo photo collage of people, events and her smiling countenance. The invitation was but a single word "all", the reply "fiat" (let it be) as she acquiesced to the invitation proffered. Two Marys shaped her life, her earthly mother, and their Mother above.

Her favorite beatitude echoes forth as a proclamation of her life and a challenge to us who remain: **"Blessed are you because you have believed!"**

Notes:

[162] On Holy Thursday 1969 Mother Celestine wrote: "The bonds of charity, between us, will be the joy, strength, salvation of the foundation... I ask the Lord that this union, between us, and with each sister may be ever more supernatural, profound and vibrant." On May 24, 1969 "il padre" wrote: "Thank you for your 'fiat/yes.' God knew us from all eternity. Our faults notwithstanding, he called us into existence to share an eternal destiny." Maria De Giorgi, pg. 142ff.

[163] Mother Bottego wrote to the sisters in Massachusetts: "See if you can help the sisters who are struggling to begin their work in Brazil and Japan. With your help they will have less material preoccupations and they will be able to work more for souls." (Feb. 1962) "Your work in Petersham has produced a great help... from this you

can understand how precious is the help that you have been able to gather together and send... The sisters in Brazil are grateful for the recent offering which you sent them." (Mar. 29, 1962)

[164] In a letter to Fr. Spagnolo from the United States Mother Bottego wrote: "I spoke with Bishop Fulton Sheen. He encouraged me and said that he was enthusiastic about the idea of our having a lay habit. He said we are the only Congregation of this kind until now. He added, it was about time to change." This letter was dated August 26, 1954, from Notre Dame, Indiana. In another letter dated September 4, 1954 Mother Bottego mentioned that a number of Directors of Propagation of the Faith offices, who were attending the Mission Congress, "shared the view of Bishop Sheen regarding our simple dress code." After attending the Mission Conference, Mother Bottego went to Maryknoll, N.Y. where she made her retreat with them and met their Foundress Mother M. Joseph, who though paralyzed continued to direct the Sisters. At Maryknoll there were 300 sisters. Maryknoll, she noted was a busy place where sisters hurried about with their work which was accompanied by a smile and joyful spirit. She was positively impressed by what she saw at Maryknoll, she defined their spirit as serene, active, and respectful. She was impressed by their religious spirit, their mission work, and their practical ways of getting things done. Mother Bottego visited the Sisters of the Sacred Heart, who were founded in France by St. Sophie Barat, in New York city and she also visited the Sisters at Villa Walsh in Morristown, N.J. She appreciated the welcome of the communities of sisters which she visited and remarked that she found the sisters in America to be as she had remembered them from her days in Butte, Montana.

[165] There are 28 Brazilian, 7 Japanese, 18 Mexican, 12 Congolese sisters among the total 239 members in the congregation at the time of the printing of this book.

[166] The Missionaries worked in Burundi from 1961-1984 and then they returned there to work in 2000.

[167] The calm has not fully returned to Sierra Leone as yet.

[168] In her letters Mother Bottego often made reference to the role of a mother and her words often give insights into her own "role of mother" within the Missionaries of Mary community. "I will remain here (Congo) as long as necessary. In the meantime I will try to pray and prepare myself to live my life as mother when I return, if God so wishes." (Jan. 24, 1960) "Your mother is closer to you (in death) than before. You should invoke her help, allow her to accompany you in your apostolic work, seek her help and counsel. If we look to the holy souls for much assistance, how much more can we expect from one who is mother." (May 30, 1961) "My doctor tells me that my recent collapse was due to tiredness, I believe that there is another cause beside tiredness, a doctor is not able to read all that is within the heart of a mother." (Apr. 7, 1962)

[169] In 1980 Fr. Amato Dagnino, s.x. a long time spiritual director of the Xaverian community and of the Missionaries of Mary offered his own timely reflections on the earlier faith matured decision of Mother to withdraw from administrative roles. "I have known Mother Celestine since 1940 when she taught English to our community. I lost contact with her in 1946, when the Missionaries of Mary, your family was born. It was 1950, I believe, when I began to regularly visit San Lazzaro and speak with Mother, every week or so with a rare faithfulness. I believe that I followed her, from then on over the past years.

Here we deal with communicating life. It is clear, understandable. Life has its moments of acute and dramatic suffering. It's to be expected. That's the way it is. Good things, profound and authentic, cannot be created without suffering, without dying. That's quite normal. If you are who you are. If you exist, you are necessarily the fruit of great affliction.

Here we are confronted with a most beautiful, sublime, significant, moment of Mother's life: when by her resignation she accepted to die beforehand. It was 1966 and Mother declared herself to be dead fourteen years before her actual death. This is true greatness. This action has a notable symbolic and prophetic value, which is the beginning of her death, that is her motherhood. Whenever a person can make a gesture of this nature, she recognizes that it's time to step aside, so others can take over. Whenever a person leaves direct generation to bury oneself in death and a hidden role, this is a sign that the person has been introduced into the luminous mystery of the Cross. This is the decisive moment.

If Mother enjoys a certain greatness among you, she appears radiant on this particular occasion. Mother has never been so truly Mother as when she accepted to die beforehand. From that moment her life moved forward in the spirit of that great biblical phrase which we repeat and meditate on almost every week: 'Unless a grain of wheat falls to the ground and dies, it remains just a grain of wheat, but if it dies, it produces much fruit'."

[170] On December 3, 1966 Cardinal Agagianian, Prefect of the S.C. of Propaganda Fide wrote to Mother Bottego: "Propaganda wishes to express it appreciation and thanks for all of the good which you have been able to accomplish until the present by your example, by your wise guidance and by your great missionary zeal... Propaganda trusts that you will assist your daughters as you wrote in your letter of April 19th, namely 'to always better understand the will of God and to seek new missionary challenges in the faith and charity of Christ'." Mother Celestine replied on December 31, 1966: "My desire to cede my responsibility in the government of our small missionary family was no act of generosity on my part... I have been aware for some time of my shortcomings, and I wished to be released from my role which had become too weighty for me. I waited for the Chapter so that the

change might take place peacefully and be accepted as an expression of the will of God... Our weakness and lack of experience notwithstanding we have witnessed the hand of God which has sustained and blessed this foundation."

[171] Mother Bottego was very concerned that work not become a priority to the detriment of the spiritual. "Be careful lest you become over tired. There is time. What you can't do this year, can be done next year." (Nov. 29, 1956) "Be firm with the principle that above all the sisters should have time for prayer and for rest. They are very generous, they will not be found lacking in the rest." (Nov. 15, 1959) "Our sisters are generous, they do not complain because of their work, however, it seems that we, as long as we are with them, should be watchful in this regard." (Jul. 25, 1954) Mother Bottego noticed during her lifetime that some other religious were kept so busy that they did not have time to pray and to rest. She did not want her sisters to fall into that pattern.

[172] Letter of Mother Bottego dated December 12, 1960 and March 7, 1961.

[173] Letter of Mother Bottego dated December 18, 1956.

[174] Vittorio Bottego, the brother of Mother Celestine, was quite angered by the seemingly unjust reduction of the Bottego lands by the city government of Parma. On the other hand, Mother Bottego regarded this misappropriation of their land with the eye of faith, and saw the benefit which might accrue to many people in need.

[175] This was a familiar saying of Blessed Marie Anne Blonens, foundress of the Sisters of St. Anne, Montreal, beatified April 29, 2001.

[176] The following are but a few expressions regarding nature in Mother Bottego's letters: "As you prepare to leave San Lazzaro and the homeland, greet it for us, greet its shores, its sky, its magnificent sun. Beauty, like goodness, remains impressed on our soul and it invites us to repeat with Keats: 'A thing of beauty is a joy forever'." (Dec. 27, 1954) "Enjoy these autumn days which will provide you with another spectacular view of the Dolomites. Fill your souls with beauty, goodness, strength to place a the service of Jesus, who will ask you for more in this coming year. 'Much will be asked of those to whom much has been given'." (Aug. 26, 1959)

[177] In a letter to Luisa Bulleri she added: "If my interior life were more intense, I would not be so remorseful for living too much for myself. Whoever loves creates, and always has something to give. I am very active by nature. At times I feel myself tied down to this small family life, my spirit seems hemmed in, and I feel weighed down." See Maria De Giorgi, pg. 58.

[178] Letter of Mother Bottego sent from Naples, to the sisters in Parma.

[179] "In these days the Lord invites us with insistence to ask, seek and obtain. Jesus assures us that the Father will hear and grant the

prayers offered in his name. I ask for nothing, I wish that through 'il padre' who guides us, you, my dearest daughters, and I may possess humility and charity."

[180] Ps 131,2

[181] Bishop Gazza, former Superior General of the Xaverian missionaries, was a native son of San Lazzaro. He had witnessed and followed the foundation of the Missionaries of Mary Community. At the funeral Mass for Fr. Spagnolo on Holy Thursday he said: "Today we commemorate in the liturgy of the supper of the Lord, the singular gesture by which Jesus wished to continue in time the work of redemption of the world. Today this action, memorial which we repeat and renew before the body of dear Fr. Giacomo, becomes an impressive liturgical coincidence which will remain for us as an indelible reference point for our lifetime."

[182] At the Good Friday Liturgy Fr. Gabriel Ferrari, Superior General of the Xaverian missionaries spoke: "This somber liturgy of Good Friday, of the passion and death of the Lord, reminds us that the seeds we place in the ground die not. All is not over. The seeds give new life, and life continues. As we consign the body of our confrere to the ground ours is a living hope. This hope stems from the cross of the One who, though innocent, died for us all. Today in the Christian world we celebrate this fact which is central to our history. Around this center we place our own little story, the story of Fr. Giacomo, all that is connected with him, because who dies with Christ, will rise with Christ. This year the fullness of the paschal mystery will be complete for him in heaven."

[183] "Easter dawns with the resplendent light and joy of the resurrection of Christ. This is my time in the desert, I am on the edge of the space which preludes eternity. Things appear in a different light, more true, more absolute, more colored by the divine. I live in the present, but my thoughts have already gone on ahead to await me in the sleep of peace. These words should not bring sadness, on the contrary they are full of great joy. They describe the direction for our temporal life. 'Here we have no lasting city, but we seek the one that is to come. If you are risen with Christ look to the things above.' This is how Easter appears to me at the present time. On the natural plane our existence apparently terminates with death. In the supernatural sphere of faith, however, the prime reason for human existence lies beyond. St. Paul assures us the resurrection of Jesus brings us to our own spiritual resurrection. This enables us to live the future reality of heaven in the joy of faith and love which constantly reflects the light of Easter, spiritually in time."

[184] "Ecclesiae Sanctae" gave norms for the implementation the Council document on the religious life.

[185] She returned on April 7th, 1968.

[186] Vittorio died on August 2, 1972. His wife, Tilde Bocchi, who survived him for ten years, died herself on August 17, 1982.

[187] These words of Mother Bottego seem to reflect what she wrote

in her Circular letter #9 dated April 24, 1963: "Our small congregation is a 'note' in the concert of the church, a note which has to vibrate perfectly within the harmonious rendition of the whole complexity, we should cooperate to guarantee that our 'note' is truly harmonious, not unlike the way various instruments in an orchestra cooperate together. In community we ought to be able to pull together and pool all of the gifts of each, seeking unity in the midst of diversity." Her words uttered on her death bed seem to reflect this thought and insist on perseverance to attain this unity with due respect for diversity.

[188] Mother Bottego left the United States when she was almost fifteen. Yet in her trip to India she wrote: "The idea that 'all men are created free and equal' is not the norm here." This observation seems inspired by the U.S. Declaration of Independence. In her circular letter of May 11th, 1965 she wrote about Our Lady and in that letter she refers to Blessed Mother as "la nostra Madre benedetta" which is also very American in contrast to the Italian "Madonna" which she customarily used. Coincidence it may be, but these seem to be phrases which date back to her early years in Butte, Montana.

[189] Concelebrants were Bishop Gazza, Bishop Tissot, Bishop Zanchin of Fidenza, Mons. Scalzotto under secretary of Propaganda Fide, Fr. Ferrari, Superior General of the Xaverian missionaries and over a hundred priests.

[190] Statement by Dr. Franco Cavazzini. See M. De Giorgi, pg. 77.

[191] Statement by Sr. Vittoria Cavazzini. See M. De Giorgi, pg. 77.

[192] When copper production was greatly diminished a group of Butte citizens joined in a project to build the Shrine of Our Lady of the Rockies. The ninety foot statue of the Virgin Mary stands on the Continental divide with hands held wide above the city of Butte below. Dauntless people created this monument to their faith and simple human values. The Shrine of Our Lady of the Rockies is quite impressive. It rests 8,000 feet above sea level, and can be seen from anyplace in Butte. A non-sectarian initiative, it is dedicated to mothers of the world. The ninety foot statue was put in place on December 20, 1985, coincidentally enough on the ninetieth birthday of Mother Celestine Bottego, foundress of the Missionaries of Mary. Our Lady of the Rockies, a hymn written by Mark Staples expresses sentiments which Mother Bottego might share: "Bless us Our Lady of the Rockies and this land those peaks divide. May our hearts be like your arms, full of love and open wide. Give us strength... Give us faith... Light our way... Hold us near... Make us all one family... Give us all one voice to sing..."

Our Lady of the Rockies Mission Statement: "To recognize the dignity of motherhood and the sacrificial love a mother has for her child, without regard to nationality or belief, in a manner that honors all women and lifts up the human spirit in love, peace and joy." This statement finds itself in part in the faith motivated selfless service of the Missionaries of Mary, founded by Mother Celestine Bottego.

CHRONOLOGY

1849?   Marriage of Bartholomew Healy (Haley) and Johanna Nally in USA.

1850?   Birth of Thomas in Ohio and in 1852? birth of James in Ohio there also.

1854   September 20th, birth of Mary in Ironton, Ohio, baptized on October 5th, in St Lawrence O' Toole's Church.

1852   Marriage of Dr. Agostino Bottego and Maria Accinelli, in Italy.

1856   Birth of Celestina, their daughter, who lived in Sicily, and died in San Lazzaro.

1858   Birth of Giovanni Battista, and in 1860 Birth of Vittorio Bottego in Parma, Italy.

1892   The Bottego family settled in Butte, Montana.

1893   August 10th, birth of Maria Bottego, Butte, Montana.

1895   December 3rd, the foundation of the Xaverian Mission Seminary, Parma, Italy by Rev. Guido M. Conforti.

        December 20th, birth of Celestine Bottego in Glendale, Ohio.

1896   January 19th, baptism of Celestine Bottego, St. Gabriel's Church, Glendale.

        October 10th, John B. Bottego became an American citizen in Butte.

1897   March 17th, death of Captain Vittorio Bottego in Africa.

        May 26th, birth of Vittorio Bottego, son of John, Butte, Montana.

1898   November 30th, baptism of Vittorio Bottego, St. Patrick's Church, by Fr. Callaghan.

1900   John Bottego, together with his children Maria and Vittorio, left for Italy. Mary H. Bottego and her daughter Celestine remain in Butte, Montana.

159

1902	Celestine Bottego was enrolled in St Patrick's school, Butte.
1906	June 3rd, Celestine Bottego received her first Communion.
1907	May 5th, Celestine Bottego was confirmed by Bishop John Carrol.
1910	Celestine Bottego graduated from St. Patrick's grammar school, she was the best student of the year in the state of Montana.
	October 10th, Mary H. Bottego and Celestine left America for Italy.
1912	January 31th, birth of Giacomo Spagnolo, Rotzo, Vicenza – Italy.
1914	September 6th, Pope Benedict XV was elected.
1916	August 23rd, Celestine graduated from the Istituto S. Vitale in Parma.
	October 31st, the Missionary Union of the Clergy was established, Bishop Conforti was President of this association from 1918-1927.
1917	November 23rd, Celestine obtained a diploma as "Teacher of English language" from the University of Pisa, Italy.
1918	November, the end of World War I.
1919	May 15th, Abbot Caronti became the Abbot of San Giovanni in Parma.
1920	July 11th, Abbot Caronti established the "Oblates of St Benedict" at the monastery of Torrechiara, outside of Parma.
1922	February 6th, Pope Pius XI was elected.
	April 27th, Celestine became a Benedictine oblate.
	October 28th, the March on Rome took place and Mussolini became head of the Italian government.
1923	Giacomo Spagnolo entered the Xaverian Institute.
1924	June 12th, Maria Bottego, sister of Celestine, entered the Franciscan Missionaries of Mary.
	Celestine Bottego began her teaching career at the Ginnasio Romagnosi of Parma.

160

1927   Maria Bottego, now Mother Maria Giovanna, left as a missionary for India.

1928   Celestine Bottego went to the University of Grenoble for advanced studies in French.

Bishop Conforti went to China to visit his missionaries there from September 19-December 28th.

1929   February 10th, the death of Mary H. Bottego, the mother of Celestine.

1932   Celestine took part in a Red Cross course for nurse's training

1934   Celestine took courses in German at the University of Innsbruck.

November 11th, Giacomo Spagnolo was ordained a priest at the age of twenty-two.

1935   Celestine Bottego began to teach English at the Xaverian Mission Seminary in Parma.

Celestine Bottego attended summer courses at the University of Strasbourg.

November 5th, death of John (Battista) Bottego, father of Celestine, San Lazzaro, Parma.

1936   July 30th, Celestine left for India to visit her sister Mother Maria Giovanna.

1938   Celestine obtained from the British Institute in Florence a certificate as a qualified and specialized in teaching of English.

1939   March 2nd, Pius XII was elected Pope.

September 1st, Germany invaded Poland.

1940   June 10th, Italy entered the war against England and France.

1941   The diocesan process for beatification was opened regarding Bishop Guido M. Conforti.

Italy declared war on the United States.

1942   In the spring, Fr. Giacomo Spagnolo began to consider the foundation of a sister community of the Xaverian Missionaries.

1943	July 2nd, Celestine Bottego was invited to take part in the foundation of the sister community of the Xaverian Missionaries. She refuses.

1943   July 2nd, Celestine Bottego was invited to take part in the foundation of the sister community of the Xaverian Missionaries. She refuses.

July 25th, the fall of Mussolini.

September 8th, the armistice with the Allies.

August 13th, Fr. Spagnolo was named Superior of the Xaverian Mission Seminary in Parma.

1944   May, part of the community of the Xaverian Missionaries transferred to Capriglio in the mountains around Parma because of air raids in the city.

In the spring, the German command took over "Villa Bottego" and Celestine went to Capriglio.

May 24th, a day of decision. Celestine Bottego accepted to cooperate with Fr. Spagnolo in the proposed foundation.

July 2nd, the men of Capriglio and the Xaverian Students were taken hostage by the Germans. They were freed the next day.

1945   May 8th, marked VE day, the end of the war in Europe.

July 19th, Teresa Danieli entered the new foundation.

September 13th the first group of the foundation transferred to Mariano.

1946   September 5th, Fr. Spagnolo was elected General Councillor of the Xaverian Missionary Congregation.

September 30th, the first group of Missionaries of Mary moved to Villa Bottego which from then on, became the Motherhouse of the nascent Congregation.

1950   July 2nd, Mother Celestine Bottego and the first three sisters made their religious profession: Teresa Danieli, Elisabetta Bellucci, Lavinia Moreschi.

1951   September 27th, the Fifth General Chapter of the Xaverian Missionaries recognized the Missionaries of Mary as their sister community.

1954   August 7th, Mother Bottego and Rosetta Serra sail for the United States, which marked the opening of the Missionaries of Mary in America.

1955   July 2nd, Bishop Colli formally established the Missionaries of Mary as a religious community within his diocese of Parma.

1956	July 2nd, Mother Bottego and the first three sisters made their perpetual profession.

1956   July 2nd, Mother Bottego and the first three sisters made their perpetual profession.

July 25th, Maria Grechi and Teresa Del Gaudio were lost in the sinking of the "Andrea Doria."

1957   May 20th, Mother Bottego, together with Gianna Lingiardi, Elisa Caspani and Anna Chiletti, left for Brazil, where a new presence was opened in the state of Paraná.

In October Cecilia Yokota and Gemma Tamura from Japan entered San Lazzaro.

1958   October 28th, John XXIII was elected Pope.

1959   August 30th, Wanda De Rosa, Maddalena Stocco, and Caterina Loi left for Japan.

1960   December 10th, Mother Bottego left for Congo with Tomasina Casali, Liliana Fantini, Rosetta Mancini and Camilla Tagliabue.

1961   January 15th, the Missionaries of Mary in Congo left for Burundi, because of the turmoil in Congo. Mother Bottego agreed to establish her sisters in Bururi on April 18th, and she herself left for Italy on April 6th.

1962   The diocese of Uvira was established in Congo, Mons. Danilo Catarzi was its first Bishop.

October 11th, marked the opening of the Second Vatican Council.

1963   June 21st, Pope Paul VI was elected.

1964   Civil war continued in Congo. All missionaries were placed under house arrest, some in May, others later in August. On October 7th, they were freed by Belgian parachutists and mercenaries.

November 12th, the Missionaries of Mary were recognized as a religious community within the Church.

1966   September 21st, the first General Chapter of the Missionaries of Mary was held.

September 24th, Mother Bottego resigned, and entrusted the congregation to her daughters.

1968   April 7th, Mother Maria Giovanna, the sister of Mother Celestine, returned to Italy after 42 years of uninterrupted service in India.

1970	January 30th, the death of Mother Maria Giovanna Bottego.
1972	August 2nd, the death of Vittorio Bottego, brother of Mother Celestine.
	September 20th, the second General Chapter of the Missionaries of Mary was held.
1978	March 22nd, the death of Fr. Giacomo Spagnolo.
	March 26th, the final common letter of Mother Bottego to her daughters.
	September 7th, the third General Chapter of the Missionaries of Mary was held.
	August 26th, the election of Pope John Paul I, who died on September 28th.
	October 16th, the election of John Paul II.
1980	August 20th, the death of Mother Celestine Bottego.
1995	April 22nd, opening of the diocesan process for the cause of beatification of the Servant of God, Mother Celestine Bottego.
1998	January 12th, the opening of the cause for the beatification of Mother Bottego by the Congregation for the Cause of Saints in Rome.

Genealogical data

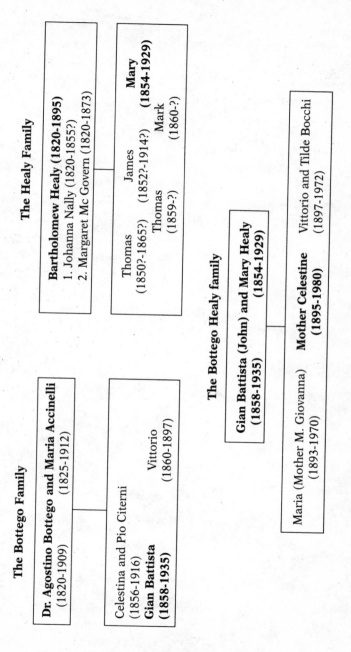

The Bottego Family

Dr. Agostino Bottego and Maria Accinelli
(1820-1909)   (1825-1912)

Celestina and Pio Citerni
(1856-1916)
Gian Battista
(1858-1935)

Vittorio
(1860-1897)

The Healy Family

Bartholomew Healy (1820-1895)
1. Johanna Nally (1820-1855?)
2. Margaret Mc Govern (1820-1873)

Thomas   James   **Mary**
(1850?-1865?)   (1852?-1914?)   **(1854-1929)**
    Thomas   Mark
    (1859-?)   (1860-?)

The Bottego Healy family

Gian Battista (John) and Mary Healy
(1858-1935)   (1854-1929)

Maria (Mother M. Giovanna)   **Mother Celestine**   Vittorio and Tilde Bocchi
(1893-1970)   **(1895-1980)**   (1897-1972)

BIBLIOGRAPHY

AMBROSE, STEPHEN E., *Nothing like it in the world*. New York: Simon & Schuster, 2000.

CLARK, MARTIN, *Modern Italy 1871-1995*. Singapore: Longmans, 1996.

CLUBBE, JOHN, *Cincinnati Observed, architecture and history*. Columbus: Ohio State University, 1992.

DALY, CHRISTOPHER, *Saint Patrick's Parish, One Hundred Years, 1881-1981*. Butte: Centennial, 1981

DE GIÒRGI, Sr. Maria, *Va' e di' ai miei fratelli, Celestina Bottego, Fondatrice delle Missionarie di Maria Saveriane*. Bologna: Editrice Missionaria Italiana, 2000 (2nd edition).

DONNELLY, JAMES S., *The great Irish Potato Famine*. England:Sutton, 2001.

DRIES, Sr. ANGELYN, OSF, *The Missionary Movement in American Catholic History*. N.Y: Orbis, 1998.

EDWARDS, R. DUDLEY & WILLIAMS, T. DESMOND, editors, *The Great Famine*. Dublin: Lilliput, 1994.

EMMONS, DAVID M., *The Butte Irish, class and ethnicity in an American Mining Town, 1875-1925*. Chicago: University of Illinois, 1990.

FOSTER, R.F., editor, *The Oxford History of Ireland*. Britain: Oxford University Press, 1989.

KEARNEY, PAT, *Butte Voices: Mining, Neighborhoods, People*. Butte:Artcraft, 1998

KILLEEN, RICHARD, *A Short History of Ireland*. England: Gill & Macmillan, 1994

LAMOTT, REV.JOHN H., *History of the Archdiocese of Cincinnati 1821-1921*. Cincinnati: Fred. Pustet,1921.

LEE, LEROY, *Our Lady builds a Statue*. Butte: 1992.

LANGEWIESCHE, WILLIAM, *The prophets of doom*. In Atlantic Monthly, April 2001.

Madre Celestina Bottego, profilo biografico e lettere circolari. Parma: Missionarie di Maria, 1981.

MALONE, MICHAEL P., *The Battle for Butte, mining and politics on the northern frontier 1864-1906.* Helena: Montana Historical Society Press, 1981.

MARSH, GEORGE D., *Copper Camp, stories of the world's greatest mining town.* (A WPA project) New York: Hastings House, 1943

MORRIS, P. F., *Anaconda Montana, Copper Smelting Boom Town on the Western Frontier.* Bethesda, MD: 1997.

PRAYER

ALMIGHTY AND MERCIFUL GOD,

you placed in the heart of Mother Celestine Healy Bottego
the burning desire that your Kingdom
be extended to the ends of the earth.
You enabled her to give herself completely
for the birth of a Missionary Family.
We ask you to glorify her on earth,
and through her intercession,
to grant us the grace we seek in faith.

Father, may your Kingdom come
soon through Mary!

Our Father, Hail Mary, Glory be.

With ecclesiastical approval

Whoever receives a grace through the intercession of Mother Celestine Healy Bottego is kindly requested to inform:

Xaverian Missionary Society of Mary
242 Salisbury Street
Worcester, MA 01609 – U.S.A.
Tel. (508) 757.0514

XAVERIAN MISSIONARIES OF MARY WORLDWIDE

United States

Mexico

Amazonia

South Brazil

United States
242 Salisbury Street
Worcester, MA 01609
Tel. 508.7570514
e-mail: xavsistersusa@aol.com

Convent of St. Jude
431 W 204th Street
New York, NY 10034
Tel. 212.5694737
e-mail: marysmission@tellurian.com

"The Missionaries of Mary find their place within the mission of the Church. They are sent to peoples and places where Christ is still unknown.
They are engaged in the initial proclamation of the Gospel, the formation of the new Christian communities, the growth and mission awareness of the local churches."

Constitution ≠ 7

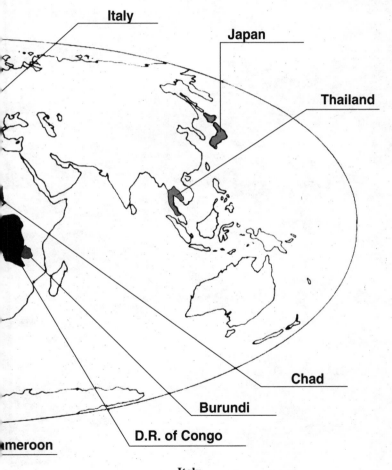

Italy

Japan

Thailand

Chad

Burundi

D.R. of Congo

Cameroon

Italy
Missionarie di Maria
Via Omero, 4 - 43100 Parma
Tel. & Fax 0521.493841
e-mail: mismadg@tin.it